Richest Lady in Town

Books by Joyce Landorf Heatherley

My Blue Blanket
The Inheritance
Unworld People
Monday through Saturday
Balcony People
Silent September
He Began with Eve
Irregular People
Joseph
I Came to Love You Late
Mourning Song
Fragile Times
Fragrance of Beauty
Changepoints

Joyce Landorf Heatherley

Richest Lady in Town

BALCONY PUBLISHING

AUSTIN, TEXAS 78734

If not otherwise indicated, Scripture quotations are from the King James Bible.

Grateful acknowledgement is expressed to the publishers for permission to quote from the following Bible translations:

The Living Bible, copyright © 1971 by Tyndale House Publishers.

The New Testament: A Translation in the Language of the People, by Charles B. Williams. Copyright © 1937 by Bruce Humphries, Inc., copyright © renewed 1965 by Edith S. Williams. Published by Moody Press.

The New Testament in Modern English. Copyright © 1958 by J. B. Phillips. Published by The Macmillan Company.

The New Testament in the Translation of Monsignor Ronald Knox. Copyright © 1944 by Sheed and Ward, Inc., New York.

The Revised Standard Version of the Bible. Copyright © 1952 by The Division of Christian Education of the National Council of the Churches of Christ in the United States of America.

Weymouth's New Testament in Modern Speech, by Richard Francis Weymouth, as revised by J. A. Robertson. Published by special arrangement with James Clarke and Company Ltd., London, by Harper and Row Publishers.

Library of Congress Cataloging in Publication Data
Heatherley, Joyce Landorf.
Richest Lady in Town.

1. Christian life -- 1960-   2. Heatherley, Joyce Landorf.
I. Title.   BV4501.2.L3183   248'.4   73-500
                 ISBN 0-929488-15-6

Printed in the United States of America

To the two most rewarding investments of my life: my all grown-up children,

Rick and Laurie

They have returned greater gains and more incredible profits than any other investment I've ever made. I am independently wealthy, more than I ever dreamed possible because of them.

ACKNOWLEDGMENTS

To these rich ladies, my creditors, my debt of thanks.

PRIS NORTON, who pushed her way through our crowded Sunday school class to ask, "Joyce, the Lord has really laid you on my heart. Can I be of any help? Could I type a rough draft or something?"

VIRGINIA SMITH, who took time off from being a wife, mother and registered nurse to give my manuscript a critic's evaluation and said revealing things like, "Joyce, you've said the same thing three times on one page. I *like* what you're saying, in fact it's the message of the entire book, but rework it and say it *once* so it has more impact!"

CLARE BAUER, who phoned long distance and usually just asked with patient love, "Joyce, haven't you finished it yet?"

SHIELA RAPP, who didn't say anything at all but simply put her husband, children and house into "planned neglect" and typed up a perfect master copy *with carbons*.

And now, for this 1992 updated edition, WENDY JUSTICE, KAREN BAKER, BARBIE WALDO, and PATTI JUSTICE, four wonderful Balcony women, who didn't hesitate a second before enthusiastically saying, "Great! When do we get to type and work on it?" And FRANCIS HEATHERLEY, my cherisher and editor.

To all of you ... Bless your darling hearts!

CONTENTS

FROM THE AUTHOR

If it had been left solely up to me, this book may not have made it back into print. But because of the visionary president of Balcony Publishing, Francis Heatherley, and the surprise of a generous financial gift from my daughter and son-in-love, Laurie and Terry Jacob, this new edition has come into being.

I have updated, added, and changed some paragraphs and pages in an effort to keep its original strengths. Yet, to be sensitive to the feelings of all, I've deleted some things as well. Also, time has passed since its first publication so I've added *Looking Back* and *The Heart of the Matter* at the close of each chapter.

Adding to all this is the soft and beautiful watercolor painting by Dennis Hill which graces the cover. "Who is she ... this lovely lady by the stream?" you ask.

Can't you tell ... ?

She's you and she's me. The richest lady in town.

ONE

Richest Lady In Town!

A millionaire lives on my street, and would you believe ... it's me! Oh, you'll never catch me strutting about in a mink-lined pantsuit, or driving around in a pale lavender Rolls Royce. In fact, I rarely think or talk about my wealth, but *I am* a bona fide, honest-to-goodness, real live heiress.

I don't have my millions tied up in trust funds, mutual funds, or future funds. I have it all right here and now. Personally, I'm irritated by people who are always bragging about their riches. That's why I've never felt I should say too much about them. But an awful thought rises in my mind. *Maybe there are a lot of people— wandering about who haven't heard about the vastness of their immense fortunes, nor do they know about their awesome, but invisible bank accounts.* I certainly didn't know about mine for a long time. Actually some years back I suspected that I had come into a fortune, but I wasn't really positive until I received official notification one Thanksgiving day.

That morning started out like any other "big dinner" day at my house. Tons of cooking, cleaning, shopping, lots of thinking, and creating went ahead of my planning because I wanted it to be special.

I was thrilled with the results. (Remember, I'm the girl who got a "D" in home economics. Twice.) My table looked like a fold-out page from the *Better Homes and Gardens* food section. The arrangement of dark burgundy and white chrysanthemums with tall, tapered yellow candles, my gleaming white china, and polished silver was the perfect setting for the dear people who sat down to "ooh" and "ahh" appropriately.

I remember where each person sat because I have several mental snap shots of them from that day. I recall my mother's face, looking puffy and pale from the chemotherapy she was going through, sending a wave of sadness through me ... my dad, hungry and, as usual, anxious to get past the turkey, etc. so he could dive into the pumpkin and mince pies he loved so much ... my sister Marilyn, two dark brown eyes sparkling and glowing with excitement at our all being together ... my husband and my beautiful children, Rick and Laurie ... my wonderful Grandpa and Grandma Uzon all dressed up in their best "Sunday-Church" clothes with expressions of delight on all their dear faces around the table. All of us missing my brother Cliff who was a Marine in Viet Nam and all of us thankful for each other. It was an unusual dinner from the start because I had never had exactly that combination of family before; and since both my mother and grandfather died within nine months of that dinner, I was never to have that blending of people again.

We asked my Grandfather Uzon to pray the blessing for the food, and in the good old Hungarian tradition, Grandpa pushed his chair back, stood up, began "Dear Lord" in English, faltered a bit, and then switched to Hungarian. I understood some of what he said, but my children didn't. It never mattered. His prayer made us all know he was talking to God and *God was listening*. We felt shivers run up our spines. After his "Amen" Grandma added her benediction of "Hallelujah," and we were ready to eat. (Actually, they were ready to eat ... I was still back on the prayer because I knew Grandpa had asked the Lord to "Bless the hands that lovingly prepared this meal." Mine!

The dinner, in my book, was a culinary delight and a smashing gourmet occasion. However, it was a success with everyone except Grandma. She could cook circles around everybody in our whole family, even the Hungarian ladies at her church, and she had little use for a dinner that didn't start out with beef or chicken soup (complete with those little farina dumplings), Hungarian chicken paprikas, and two other meat dishes (with hand-made noodles this time), and end up with her *rétes* and strudel (dainty, tissue-paper thin dough surrounding apples, cinnamon, and nuts). My baked acorn squash with its buttery pecan syrup sauce didn't sit very *Hungarian* with her, but she was a good sport and picked her way around it. Later, at home in her own kitchen she probably cooked up a batch of food for Grandpa to fill him up and to make amends for my American-style feast.

I don't recall too much of the conversation that glorious day other than that we laughed a great deal, and the dinner time stretched into two-and-a-half noisy, wonderful hours.

It was after the last pieces of pumpkin and mince pie had disappeared, while I was cleaning the last bit of spilled gravy off my white tiled sink that I worked alone in the kitchen with my husband. I moved my mother and grandma out of the kitchen into the living room, and as I was carefully fitting the leftover turkey into our overcrowded refrigerator we got the great news!

My grandfather had vanished from sight right after dinner and without my knowledge had taken his own personal tour of our house, garage, and backyard and had ended up in the kitchen. His arms were folded over his fat tummy and there was a contented smile on his face.

To my husband, and in his fractured English, Grandpa said with an old wise man's authority,

"You know vat?"

"What, Grandpa?"

"You," he shook his finger, "You are millionaire!"

There was a small laugh of protest out of my husband, and he patted Grandpa's shoulder and mumbled something about that not being true. He intended to end Grandpa's conversation, but as Grandpa had looked our house over he had given his speech considerable thought and was not about to be shushed.

So Grandpa straightened to his full height and said, "You listen. I tell you da trute. You are big millionaire. You got this house, you got children, you got her." Now he was wagging his finger under my husband's nose.

"And you know *vat else*?" Grandpa was almost shouting. I think it was because he didn't want either of us to miss his punch line:

"You millionaires. *You got God!*"

Both of us were instantly struck by the profound truth of Grandpa's words. In fact, it seemed the truth clanged so loudly it was almost deafening.

Then my husband put his arms around dear, wise, old Grandpa and said in a loving tone, "You're right, Grandpa. You're right!"

It was a year later that I began the first draft of the book *His Stubborn Love*—the story of the making of a millionaire. Months after Grandpa died, I remembered his incredible announcement the last Thanksgiving day we were together, "*You are mil-lionaires!*"

You see, I *am* the richest lady in town, not because of hoarded cash, immense investments in stocks and bonds, an heirloom collection of jewelry, or vast property holdings, but because of God's outpouring of spiritual wealth. I have at my fingertips large holdings of spiritual gifts, treasures, and yes, even power, working and readily available in me. You do too, if you belong to Christ. In fact, we have "far more than we would ever dare to ask or even dream of—infinitely beyond our highest prayers, desires, thoughts, or hopes!" (Eph. 3:20, *Living Bible*)

So, come on, leave whatever you're doing and go to the bank with me. I know the folks at the bank and I'll introduce you to everyone. After that, I'll sign you into the safe deposit area and together we will peek into the box of treasured riches! Some of the greatest values are found in the "Talent Account" (it always surprises me); the "Gentleness Account" (it instantly connects me with the Lord!); and the "Refinement Account" (I'd *rather* do without this one, yet each time I draw on it I wouldn't take a million dollars for the experience)—these and other accounts are all available to you and me. They are at our fingertips, ready and waiting for us to do our own taking.

What's that? You don't think you've got any such accounts? Oh, yes, you do. It's probably just that no one has ever pointed out your bonanza of wealth. In fact, you may have *more* than I do; and that's just fine with me, but what a shame it would be to live your life without the knowledge of your legacy!

You'd be like the people we read about in the newspapers every now and then. "Older woman dies of starvation ... one hundred thousand dollars found under her mattress." "Man died in filth and squalor of tenement building. Fifty thousand dollars and stocks worth a half million were found in his kitchen drawer."

What a preposterous situation! Yet almost every day I meet Christians who are convinced they are destitute and penniless, when in reality they are quite wealthy.

Once while I was writing this book, as I sat in the den-tist's chair waiting for the final numbness to set in, the dental assistant asked me what I was writing. (Now, that's a danger-ous question to ask a writer because it really turns on the flow of words.) So I began to tell her about this book and I said, "You know, even though you are a young widow with five children, Diane, you are wealthy because you are God's woman with immense riches."

Her eyes filled with tears, and she said, "Oh, Joyce, I needed to be reminded of that. I'm so bogged down with the problems of working and raising my children that I had forgotten how *very* rich I am!" Then she spent a few more minutes encourag-ing me to finish this book quickly.

If you are a Christian and you truly don't feel wealthy, try reading Ephesians 1. It tells of our remarkable legacy. Phrases like, "In Him too we have been made heirs" (v. 11, Weymouth's translation); "stamped with the promised Holy Spirit as a guarantee of purchase" (v. 13, Phillips' translation); the Holy Spirit "is the first installment of our inheritance" (v. 14, Williams' translation) show that you are wealthy whether you remember your back accounts or not.

This book has not been written to tell you how I *found* my first million before I was forty years of age, but rather, how I've learned to *spend* it! Read on!

Read the calm and confident words of David,

Psalm 16:5-6
Lord, you have assigned me my
portion and my cup;
You have made my lot secure.
The boundary lines have fallen for me
in pleasant places;
Surely, I have a delightful
inheritance.

LOOKING BACK

I can still see those dear faces on that Thanksgiving day in the mid-sixties.

I can still hear darling Hungarian Grandpa Uzon announcing as proudly as if he was saluting the American flag that he loved so much, "You millionaires!"

And even though both Grandpa and Grandma Uzon, my mother and father are all with the Lord now...and time has wrought many changes and transitions since that day, Grandpa is still right. I *am* a millionaire!

HEART OF THE MATTER

Actually, whatever we have or do not have, and no matter who is taken from us, this fact remains solid:

Our heavenly Father "owns the cattle on a thousand hills," and if he notes even the sparrow's fall, surely he sees and takes loving care of us. Most certainly, we have inherited riches upon riches as his children.

We *are* millionaires.

TWO

The Talent Account

The first account I'd like you to see is a large multifaceted one called "Talent." And before you skip lightly through it thinking, "This account is not for me because I don't *have* any talent," let me tell you of an experience I had some years ago.

I was honored to be singing and speaking for the Protestant Women of the Chapel at the Army's Sukiran Chapel in Okinawa. At the beginning of my program, I said that after I sang I would be talking about talent. But even as I announced it, I felt someone, perhaps many, would hear the word "talent" and think, *"Well, that lets me out—I'm not talented at all!"*

I was counting on the Lord to really speak through me since many women (myself included) have the problem of low self-esteem at some level. Some of us really believe we are of no value, or at best, of little worth as human souls.

One of the first women to reach me after the meeting was a lovely lady whose eyes were sparkling and glistening with tears.

"You know, Joyce," she began, "when you said the word 'lent' today, I almost got up and walked out because if there is one thing I don't have, it's *talent*. But I decided to stay anyway. I'm so glad I did. As I listened to you, it seemed as if God was pointing out one talent after another in my life ... I had no idea they existed. I was deeply moved and convicted. I've asked the Lord to forgive me for not recognizing them, and I've come out of this meeting feeling that I just may be far more needed and useful in this life than I dreamed. I'm looking forward to fulfilling some new life goals."

She was not the only woman who came to the meeting feeling inadequate and untalented. Many of us honestly believe we have *no* God-given talent and, of course, that deeply affects *our* perception of who we are as women.

A minister once told me that 50 percent of the women he counseled in his office were there because of their feelings of having no worth, no talent, or no real purpose in living.

Women, not only on an Army base in Okinawa, but all over the world have fallen into the common trap of defining talent as *only* the ability to play the piano, to sing, or to paint lovely oil paintings, when in reality, talent is having a natural, God-given ability to do something, *anything*, well.

You might ask, "Great, what are the 'somethings I do very well' in *my* life?"

Here is a list of just a few examples:

1. The talent to be cheerful. Particularly when nothing is going right, you've spent the day errand-chasing all over town, and everyone has been less than nice.
2. The talent to be hospitable. To open your home and entertain angels (or teenagers) even though your couch is threadbare, the living room needs painting, or you just began payments on white carpeting in your living room. (Time proved that when my kids were teenagers the white carpet I chose for my living room was not one of my swiftest decorating moves. Oh well, *I* enjoyed it. For a while.)
3. The talent to know how to affirm and demonstrate your love for your loved ones. Even though you know, better than most, all their foibles and faults.

4. The talent to speak your mind with loving tact. I know a woman who, if she wanted to, could give you a "bawling out" with such tact you wouldn't realize it until three weeks later. That's real talent!

5. The talent to take a course in oil painting, sewing, or business and *finish* it, or the talent to go back to school and graduate or get a degree. Now this requires the talent of self-discipline!

6. The talent to upholster your own chair, add unique buttons to a ready-made dress, or take a Simplicity, Jiffy pattern and make baby sacks for the missionary project even though sewing a straight seam has never been your strong point.

7. The talent of being on time. It seems to me that the busier life gets, the more we miss deadlines, appointments and schedules. I'm not suggesting that we arrive early for anything—but being *on time* is a whole lot better than being *late*. However, the talent to be on time is a rare one today.

8. The talent of communicating love *without* words. Doing it by a look, a pat on the arm, a smile, or just taking the *time* to lovingly look at a child's drawing.

9. The talent of finding out what "pleasures" each member of your family and *doing* it on a regular basis. When my son, Rick, was growing up he used to love chocolate pudding cake. Now that he is almost forty years old, it still gives me joy to make it for him and his family as I did on a recent visit with them. Laurie always liked the way I decorated our homes. Now that she has her own family and home, I delight in "re-doing" rooms for her ... like this past week when my grandson James' room got a new fresh look and I got to staple up sheets on the walls in the kids' bathroom. My husband LOVES my macaroni and cheese. No, actually he LOVES everything I cook. So it makes cooking a pleasurable

thing for me. Actually, it's a beautiful experience to give my family pleasure; to know *what* makes them happy, and then go ahead and do it.

10. The talent of listening when someone speaks. An astonishing number of people never heard of this talent, but once you find a friend talented in this direction, you never get over it! You stand in awe of him or her and your love for this friend becomes an ever deepening experience.

11. The talent of watching how your children throw down their school books and praying to God for wisdom in asking, "Hi, Honey, how was school today?" Motherhood is no easy trick nor is it thoughtlessly done. I've come to realize how very talented my mother was with all her children and am not surprised that my sister Marilyn, who has four daughters and one son, has inherited our mother's talent of wisdom.

12. The talent to make lumpless gravy like my mother-in-law Margaret used to do and Laurie's mother-in-law, Evelyn, does now.

These are twelve talents that popped into my mind with only casual effort. There are many, many more. Did you find one of yours? If not, make your own list. The talents are endless. Let's go back for a moment to the first talent, the talent of being cheerful.

It's easy to be cheerful and kind to lovely, easy-to-get-along-with people. But if God has given you this talent, you'll have high adventure just on an average day of going to school, to work or shopping, banking or running errands. The opportunities to be cheerful are endless!

The big joy of this talent is the powerful Christian witness it gives to those around you and those you interact with during the day.

For a number of years I was actively engaged in presenting Christ to two checkers and three box boys at the supermarket and to three or four tellers at the bank. I prayed for them regularly and dearly coveted their souls for God—though some of them had no idea that for years their names had been on my daily prayer list. Each time I was with them I prayed, smiled and listened very carefully (not necessarily in that order), and God produced some special miracles in several of their lives. Now it's true, he used my first book in one case, but other than that, my singing and piano-playing talents were not called upon. In fact, never once during these three years of shopping or banking did I wheel in my piano and say, "Have I got a treat for you! I'm going to use my vocal and piano talent that God has given to me as a witness to you." Nor did I jump up on the checkout counter to sing a few numbers and *use those talents*! In fact, some of the very ones who were reached in those years by our heavenly father *never* did hear me sing, and it's quite conceivable they never did know of my "other" talents.

The talents they did see were of a quite different nature. Those other talents began with my coming up to the checkout counter at the supermarket and beating the checker at saying, "Hi, how are you today?" She was paid to be polite. I wasn't.

One day at the bank after I said first, "Hello, how are you today?" the teller put down her pencil, shook her head, and said, "Joyce, you are something else! You aren't like any other Christian woman I've ever know."

I wasn't sure exactly how to take that, so I asked, "How do you mean?"

"You always radiate" (she stumbled for words here because she was in unfamiliar territory) "uh, Christian love. If I didn't know you were religious I would never have guessed you to be a Christian. You're cheerful, kind, and have a sense of humor."

"You mean other Christians don't?" I asked.

"Not when they come in here," she snapped.

What a sad commentary on us as Christians!

The talent for being cheerful, smiling, and pleasant even when it's raining buckets of problems is the talent Paul and Silas had ... particularly when they *sang* in prison! It was a God-given ability that had them singing in spite of their prison experience.

It's highly possible that if your talent is being cheerful or one of the others on my list, you may never become famous. My mother was a classic example of this. She died in 1966, when she was in her late fifties. She was never published (although she left me volumes of her written thoughts, and was never a household word among women, yet her influence then with people and her influence now continues to shape and mold me and countless thousands even today. So remember, books may not be written about your life; songs may never be sung or dedicated to you; but the God who sees and knows all things keeps perfect records. He does not classify your special ability of being a great cook, knowing how to bake apricot pie, balancing a checkbook, dressing a skinned knee, raising, teaching, and training children, being a librarian, a lawyer, a doctor, a minister, a secretary, a clerk, or a professional business woman as non-talents.

On the contrary, through Paul we have these words, "I can never stop thanking God for all the wonderful gifts he has given you, now that you are Christ's: he has enriched your whole life...Now you have every grace and blessing; every spiritual gift and power for doing his will are yours during this time of waiting on the return of our Lord Jesus Christ" (1 Cor. 1:4, 5,7, *Living Bible*).

We tend to get all hung up with our preconceived ideas as to *which* talents are really important, and in the confusion it is highly possible to miss God's plan for our lives.

When my son Rick was still a teenager, a friend asked him how it felt to have such a beautiful and talented mother. I loved his answer because he mentally tossed aside "beautiful and talented" and came up with, "I think she's great, but you should taste her chicken and dumplings." (Ah yes, the way to a man's heart ...)

I really appreciated Rick's answer, partly because the "talent" of making chicken and dumplings came *after* long practice, but mainly because it told me that in his mind my cooking was just as great, if not greater, than my talent as a singer, broadcaster, or writer.

Perhaps you can't possibly think of cooking chicken and dumplings as a talent. However, I think it takes enormous talent to just be a woman today. If it doesn't, why are so many marriages unraveling at the seams? If it takes no talent to bake a great pie, why is it so many homes and restaurants serve such inferior pies...or none at all? If it doesn't take talent to raise children, why are abuse and crimes against children spiraling upward? If it doesn't take talent to be a Sunday school teacher, why does the superintendent keep pleading for more teachers and workers all the time?

Yes, I *am* oversimplifying it a bit, but you do get the message, don't you? It takes *talent* to do what might be classified as an "ordinary task" with any degree of expertise.

Think about your own life for a moment. Isn't there something special you do that certainly could be listed as a talent?

After hearing me say this, a young mother and friend of mine nodded her head knowingly and said, "Let me tell you, the mother who just listens to her child practicing the piano and is able to keep her sanity and sense of humor at the same time is displaying a great deal of God-given talent!"

I can still picture another woman who came up to me at the same meeting in Okinawa when I'd talked on talents. She said to me, "Oh, sure you *know* what talents he's given you, but God's never told me what mine are and I'm fifty-one years old, so it's a little late to find out."

Are you married?" I asked.

"Yes," she answered.

"Any children?"

Almost nonchalantly she tossed off, "Yes, I've eight kids."

"Eight? Excuse me? You have eight kids? Tell me about them."

"They're really all marvelous kids," she answered. "Some are married, some single. A couple have gone into medicine and are doctors. Two are ministers and one daughter is a missionary."

I was stunned. I wanted to shout, "Are you kidding? You're standing in front of me saying in effect, 'Poor me, I don't have *any* talents,' when you have produced and nurtured eight fabulous, worthwhile human beings who are being a credit to God and the human race?"

Instead I just blurted out, "Don't tell me that didn't take talent! Or did your kids just grow up like weeds without water or cultivation? Didn't you feed and clothe them physically, mentally, and spiritually? Didn't you lovingly discipline and correct them? Didn't you give them praise, love and the benefit of God's wisdom? Didn't you pay for voice, piano, and clarinet lessons? And then listen and watch over all that practice time? Isn't all that being a 'professional mother' just as in my singing and playing I am called a 'professional musician'?" Who dares say that raising children, surrounding them with a loving and a safe home life doesn't take talent?

I pray that we, especially as Christian women, will allow God to make us teachable so we will see the unique talents he's given all of us for this world in which we live. You may not be rich in *my* talents, but I'm not rich in yours either. All talents are from God. It's what we do with them that really makes them outstanding.

Do you remember the little boy who gave Jesus his lunch of five loaves and two fishes? It was hardly enough to feed himself and a friend, much less the thousands who were there that day, yet the boy *gave what he had*. From that point ... the point of surrendering what he had ... Jesus did the rest!

Let's not sit back in the comfort of the rut called denial and say we have no talent; rather let's ask God to use what we already have. Let's ask God to make us vitally aware of the special abilities he may choose to develop...those talents that were within you, all along, just waiting for the spark of God's creative touch to ignite and burst into being.

Now, let's say that in these past moments God has truly revealed some of the areas in your life where you do have special abilities. How do you handle it? Do you become super-conceited or piously humble? What should your attitude be?

The key that really opens up the Talent Account is an unlikely one found in the Beatitudes.

I had never looked at the Beatitudes or thought much about my own connection to them until I read a marvelous piece of writing called *The Beatitudes for Women* by my friend, Colleen Evans.

I sang and spoke at the First Presbyterian Church of La Jolla, California, where at that time Colleen's husband, Louie Evans was pastor. Each plate at the luncheon held a copy of her *Beatitudes*. The booklet gave me a glimpse of an account loaded with resources, so I began to study seriously those remarkable words of Jesus.

The Beatitude that grabbed my heart as far as talent is concerned was the one about being humble. The Phillips translation says: "How happy are the humble-minded." No other word in Christian circles is so subject to individual interpretation as "humble." Sermons about being humble go from one extreme to another. One preacher stresses we are all "worm-like" and totally unworthy. The next pastor tells us we are *powerful*, "we can do all things", and that only muddies up the water. I got tired of wondering just how we were to be balanced about being humble, so I began searching the scriptures for the guidelines God has given us.

It seems to me that often the word "humble" is linked with our having a talent. It's almost as though if we don't have a talent then humility is not going to be one of our problems. But we all need a sense of humility in our lives; as it acts like a lens to bring things into proper focus.

As Colleen Evans said: "She is a happy woman who knows that without God she is *nothing! But with God* she has great potential and strength!"

We don't have to have an inferiority complex. We don't have to bogg down on the words to that old hymn "... for such a worm as I ..." Listen, darling women, God paid a fantastic price for us, though, as a matter of fact, He didn't owe us a thing! He could have left us stumbling around, wading through one problem after another, living one horrible, unjust day after another; but by God's great, stubborn love, he has *chosen* to care, to buy back, to give Himself to us and to bless each of us with *talents!*

I know perfectly well that God has given me the ability to sing; and I know equally well I have no talent at fixing my own hair. I know, too, that I can cook Hungarian stuffed cabbages (Töltö Kaposzta) to perfection and that I have mastered three chords on the guitar, though a fourth won't come through my fingers no matter how hard I practice. What am I saying? Just this: I know my abilities and I know my limitations. The moment I confuse or distort these facts, humility goes out the window.

The first time I sang a real grown-up solo in my Dad's church, I was thirteen years old. I did, as my mother succinctly put it, "a good job." After the service three older ladies approached me. One woman began with, "My dear" (right there was my first clue. I knew I was going to get it). They said nothing about my song or the way I sang it ... they just pulled themselves up, towered over me and declared, "We are going to pray that God keeps you humble." In light of many things that have happened in the years since—I suspect those ladies are still alive and probably praying the same prayer!

It may have been the first left-handed compliment I ever heard. Their words lifted me up and slapped me back down in one short sentence. Those ladies, besides the rejection I felt, put me into the position of feeling as if I should apologize for the talent I believed (and had been told by my mother) God had given me. So from then on, when people *did* praise my singing, I'd go into my newly learned behavior response and say, "Oh no, thank you, but I can't sing at all. Really, I've so much to learn, etc ... etc." I was hoping they'd think I was genuine *and*, oh yes, humble.

It wasn't until after I had grown up a bit that I dropped the false humility mode and accepted and dealt with the fact that it was God who had given me a voice ... and that some people, upon hearing it, even heard and felt the touch of the Lord through my music. When they complimented me, I could honestly be balanced enough to say, "Thank you, isn't the Lord marvelous!" Without Him I'm nothing, true, but I'm *not without* Him. I'm *with* Him.

Paul helped tremendously with my attitude regarding talent when he said, "Try to have a sane estimate of your capabilities" (Rom. 12:3 Phillips' translation).

There it is, two thousand years old and right on target. A *sane estimate*.

I have long observed that very few of us women have a "sane estimate" of our talents or of our lives in general. That same verse in the Amplified Bible reads, each one rating "his abilities with sober judgment," never underestimating or *over*estimating.

The opposite of being humble is being conceited! I've known several musicians who were this way, and their behavior on and off stage was extremely temperamental because of it. But, that kind of conceit is an *obvious* kind. I'd like to write about the subtle kind of conceit that inhabits some women (and men) today. They are the women who seem to have a deep need within them to control and dominate the lives of other people.

A group of us had dinner once with one such woman. She told us what restaurant we'd attend, where to park, and where to wait before we were seated. Her husband stood quietly by, minding his p's and q's and trying not to get in the way. She ordered the food for each of us and after the meal told us when we could leave. She was in her eighties and did all of this with a semi-gracious charm, but that did not disguise the fact that she felt she knew everything there was to know *about* everything. She turned off everyone else's ideas, thoughts, and opinions. She simply had to have the final say. She had so exaggerated her own talents and abilities that her conceit had developed into control, and the absence of humility made her extremely unattractive.

What a waste, I recall thinking. She was intelligent and had some eighty years of experience she could have shared with us; but she was so busy calling all the shots and making people jump on command that we never really got to know her.

What all of us could use in our relationships with others is the lovely balance of Paul's words to form our own "sane estimate of our capabilities." We need to be balanced and honest in seeking how to handle our talents.

When I first wrote this chapter, years ago, I was at Hume Lake Christian Camp Grounds in the beautiful mountains above Fresno, California. I was speaking at a Women's Auxiliary tea, and I departed from my usual speaking arrangements to ask them if I could share a part of a new book I was writing (this one). They couldn't very well object (smile), so I began giving my ideas about humility and invited them to give me their ideas.

Afterward a gifted woman, Bobby Romis, said she'd like to share one thought with me.

Bobby opened her Bible to the familiar passage in Proverbs 31 on "the virtuous woman." When she got to the eighteenth verse she said, "While you were talking about humility and talent I remembered this verse, 'She perceiveth that her merchandise is good: her candle goeth not out by night. She layeth her hands to the spindle, and her hands hold the distaff!'" Then Bobby looked up from her reading and said, "What a woman! As she appraised her own merchandise, she knew (no apologies and no bragging) that it was good." The balance of a *sane estimate* is obviously here.

Bobby continued, "In other words, this Proverbs woman would be the one who would accept the chairmanship of the Hume Lake Country Fair. She would know how to do it and she would set up committees involving the best women she could find. She would work far into the night to make the Country Fair a success ['... her candle goeth not out by night ...'] and when the fair was over, she'd know her 'merchandise was good' and she'd go home and spin wool!

"Look at her. She goes home from being a brainy, hard-working chairman of the Hume Lake fair to spinning wool. She is not insulted at the change in status, no 'poor me' spirit; and because spinning wool takes no mind-bending efforts, she probably takes that time to pray for her husband, children, and her own business interests. What a woman! She knows her talents are good, stays up to carry them out, and is beautifully able to be home spinning wool the following day."

Bobby finished by saying, "I feel God has set up a pattern for us in these verses: honestly knowing our outside-of-the-home talents; working hard and bringing them into completion; and then, even with the problems of readjusting, having a routine day in the home. We need a time to sit, or to be quiet and, yes, even to sew, iron, and do dishes—using that time to renew our *own* strength and to pray for the dear members of our family."

As Bobby finished her thoughts on this pattern of balance, I thought of the endless number of times I've given concerts, spoken to several hundred women, or counseled with a woman or a teenager, and then came home to the quiet of my sewing room, turned on my iron, and prayed over the clothes as I've ironed them.

One of my favorite humorous writers, Erma Bombeck, said she got her best ideas for her writing over the ironing board. I know how that works, except that with me, I've always done my best praying over an ironing board.

I've had years of practice at praying over a shirt, a blouse, a pair of pants or a dress. I've prayed over collars and the stressed-out neck muscles they would be covering. I've prayed for sleeves that would hold an arm that must do so many things. And whenever I got to a front panel of a shirt, blouse, or dress, I'd pray loving prayers for the heart that would beat beneath the fabric. It was particularly delightful to pray over Rick's or Laurie's clothes as I ironed them—besides it made a boring task a tad more interesting, and in those quiet moments of household meditation I think I grew in stature and my loved ones benefitted from it. Who's to say that singing a whole concert, writing a book or giving a public speech takes *more* talent than the ironing? Not I!

This whole chapter on talent can be summed up in one exciting verse: "God has given each of you some special abilities; be sure to use them to help each other, passing on to others God's many kinds of blessing" (1 Peter 4:10, *Living Bible*).

If we say we have no special abilities, we are either in denial or calling God a liar. If our motives in being used are not to help each other, then we think talent is only singing or playing piano, and we rob ourselves and others of "God's many kinds of blessings."

Our living in this twentieth-century world does not have to be a boring, worthless, "nothing" type of existence. It can be the door to real, creative living, the hinges of which are oiled with a "sane estimate of our capabilities."

We need to start right now; it's never too late. We can quit the tired old routine of "poor me, I have no talents" and begin to take a good look at ourselves and own unique talents and abilities.

While it may not take too much effort to convince you that your singing talents aren't too great, you just may find an extraordinary personal skill in your kitchen staring down into the gravy skillet, or at your job talking out loud to your computer. Do you know what talent lumpless gravy requires? Or maybe the computer is just your cup of tea, and you are presently discovering a talent you never knew you had! (Not me. I still find telephones a puzzlement, so I'm always going to write my books in long hand.)

Remember the lady in Okinawa? The one with "I don't have any talents...just eight kids?" Well I know for a fact that on that day, after hearing that we all have special gifts and abilities, that woman asked the Lord to reach down and touch her vision so she could clearly see her talents. She didn't go right out and buy herself a piano so she could begin to play and sing. She simply went home, sensing with new joy her *own* worth and value and knowing a little bit more about her *own* talents. She was a beautiful woman before the service that day, but she carried herself taller and was positively radiant *after* the meeting.

We can all experience the same joy and radiance, the same feeling of self-worth she received if we'll just let God open our eyes to our very *our own* special abilities and talents.

LOOKING BACK

From the age of three I just knew I'd be a singer when I grew up. All my energy and training went in that direction. Yet, I've ended up as primarily a woman who is a writer and speaker and who merely ends most programs with a song.

HEART OF THE MATTER

We shouldn't be surprised at the way God channels our talents, expands them, or, out of the blue, brings out in us a talent we never knew we had!

THREE

The Gentleness and Mercy Account

I might never have found the "Gentleness and Mercy Account" had it not been for a mother, two little boys, and the Alpha Beta Market on the corner ... but I'm ahead of my story.

Let me start by saying that from my early thirties on I really wanted to be God's woman. So I tried, with all my might and mind, to listen to Godly people, to read every book I could lay my hands on, but mostly I began a serious search of God's Word to find patterns, clues, and His directions for my life. (I had followed my own pattern, clues, and directions for a few years and never, *never* did I want to go back to that rather catastrophic way of living!) However, every once in a while in the Bible I'd come across a scripture that made absolutely no sense at all to my twentieth-century mind and life. I'll never forget one such verse. There I was quietly minding my own devotions one morning, reading along in Paul's letter to the Philippians when I came to the words, "Let your moderation be known unto all men" (Phil. 4:5).

My eyes read on but my mind stayed behind and began to boggle a bit. So, I re-read it, "Let your moderation be known unto all men." What in the world, what in *my* world did that mean? In the first place, "moderation" simply does not describe me. I'm rarely moderate about anything. If the chicken is absolutely delicious, it is *absolutely* delicious, not merely well done. If my hair is a mess, take it from me, it's a mess and *not* somewhere in between. Add to this the fact that part of me is Hungarian and the other part Irish, and being outspoken is a normal trait like having one head, one body, two arms, and two legs. My first thought on that verse was, "Well, I'm sure glad Paul wasn't talking to me, because I'll never be a moderate, middle-of-the-road person."

As I thought about that, I had this mental picture: a Christian living his whole life in moderation, walking in the middle of the road, having no outspoken opinions, never making other people happy, sad, angry or anything. It was not possible for me to see myself as a most non-active type of person. I'm just too noisy, too outspoken, too alive to be boxed-in to moderation. So ... I dismissed the notion.

However, in the days that followed, that verse would not lie down and be quiet. It kept popping back into my mind, particularly when I felt the need to yell an opinion at Rick or Laurie or voice a strong thought to my husband.

Later that week, since some of my dearest friends are ministers, I thought I'd phone one of them and ask how that verse could be applied to me. But it never seemed to be the right time, and more often than not I'd pass the phone, go out to the garage and put my washed clothes into the dryer. One morning I got to thinking about "direct dialing" and decided to go straight to the top and ask the Lord. The instructions I thought I heard in my mind sounded like I should read some other translations, so that's where I began.

After much searching I was *convinced* Paul wasn't talking to me. I kept finding words like "forbearance" and "consideration," and since these are not necessarily among my stronger points, I was about to give up when I looked at one final translation. It was so on target I think I know exactly how Goliath would have felt if he could have reviewed the incident just after David did his thing with his trusty sling!

Phillips' translation read, "Have a reputation for gentleness." A reputation for gentleness? *Who, me?* I thought. *No, gentleness will never be a word to describe me after I'm gone.*

In *Spirit-controlled Temperament*, Tim LaHaye discussed the four basic human temperaments: the sanguine, the choleric, the melancholic and the phlegmatic.

If you read his book you probably identified with one or two of those traits. You may also have found that he accurately pegged your husband's personality too. I found my own temperament in the middle of the outgoing, talkative, sanguine temperament with some of the drive and ambitions of the choleric thrown in ... and, hovering over me, a cloud called melancholy. Since I identified more with the sanguine than the others, I was very interested in reading everything he had to say about them.

Tim's next book, *Transformed Temperaments*, dealt with St. Paul, the choleric, Moses, the melancholic, Abraham, the phlegmatic, and the sanguine of all sanguines, St. Peter.

Peter had all the traits typical to the sanguine personality—talkative, bold, friendly, and outgoing. He was loved yet seemed always to march in where angels feared to tread. Tim LaHaye described him as having a tendency toward being rough and impatient. Much like the proverbial "bull in the china shop." So the command to gentleness gave Peter and all us sanguines a real challenge! In fact, perhaps the only hope for us loud, talkative, highly opinionated people is to be transformed by the presence of the Holy Spirit in our lives.

Somehow I'd mislaid that lovely redeeming fact about the Holy Spirit. I'd forgotten what a beautiful work the Holy Spirit can do, given any kind of chance. I only knew I was in trouble. *I was not gentle, and furthermore, I didn't see the importance of being gentle, and I felt it was too late in life to get a reputation for it.* I tried to dismiss the verse. But during the day it clung to my consciousness, and it must have wandered in and out of my subconscious thoughts at night because I'd wake in the morning with a print out of the verse across my mind.

I must have mulled and stewed over that verse and the gentleness bit for weeks. Then something that sounded remarkably like what my mother would have said rang loud and clear: "Joyce-honey, now that you've tried other things, you *might* ask the Lord about it."

So, one morning while I was mentally ruminating over this verse, and having a second cup of coffee, I prayed,

Dear Lord, You *know* (because You made me) gentleness is not exactly my life style. Actually, if I were really honest with You, Lord, I'd have to say I haven't really cared about even wanting gentleness in my life. I figure it's a lost cause—why work on it when it's such a tremendous impossibility? It takes too much time and thought to be gentle, and frankly, I'm too tired to put forth the effort.

But, Lord, it seems to me that You have gone to great lengths to capture my attention on this subject, and I can't ignore the fact that You seem eager to teach me this rare and difficult art. You *do* have Your work cut out for You. I'm not coming into this learning program with very much confidence! You've done some great miracles in my life, but I don't see how I'll ever learn. Will You be *most* specific, and, remembering my frail mind, give me some down-to-earth, practical illustration?"

Then that strangely familiar realization happened as it sometimes does during prayer. Though no clear cut illustration was given to me, I felt the Lord had answered me. So I left the prayer about gentleness with him.

The next day I went grocery shopping to get out of the house, and I forgot entirely about gentleness. I applied myself to the task of figuring out how to fill the teenaged "bottomless pits" I lived with.

The Alpha Beta market was about five blocks from our house. There was nothing particularly religious about its building, parking lot, products, checkers, or box boys, except that one box boy was my son, Rick, who, come to think of it, had a whole lot of qualities that were (and still are) remarkably Christ-like. But, for all practical purposes, that market and its people were just fine for selling groceries, but they were not well known for teaching theology.

It was late Saturday afternoon by the time I arrived. As you know, there couldn't be a worse time to shop, and I hadn't been able to con anyone into going with me to push my basket or give me moral support as I spent all that money. So, there I was, bored and miserable, pushing my cart, and trying to get the whole thing settled in the shortest amount of time possible.

The problem of racing the clock was aggravated by a roadblock in the first aisle. I couldn't get around a certain shopper no matter *how* I maneuvered. She was a young, beautiful blonde with two cute little boys. One must have been all of four or five and the other not quite two. From the top of her super-sized pink rollers down to her sandals, the mother seemed near the edge of hysteria.

I put it all together like this: She had been thinking earlier that afternoon that she'd wash her hair that night, clean up the house later, and do her grocery shopping on Sunday when, out of the blue, her husband called and said, "Honey, the boss and his wife are coming for dinner tonight."

At least that's what I suspected had happened because she was about as calm as a volcano on the verge of erupting. The boys were "helping" her by handing her this can or that package, and she was trying not to scream as she put each item back on some shelf. (I thought of Rick stocking those same shelves later and how most likely he'd wonder how in the world that sack of sugar got mixed in with the dill pickles.) The boys were having a fine time. They climbed in and out of the basket and once the little one got into mine. I handed him back and said, "I believe this belongs to you?" She just took him and rolled her eyes toward the ceiling in a way most helpless mothers do.

By now we had worked our way through half the store, and

I continued frantically to try to get past and ahead of her. No
way! Then, when we headed for the wide meat aisle, hope
soared within me. I thought, *Aha! I'll cut her off at the pass!* So,
I maneuvered, raced, picked up less meat than I intended, and
barreled through shoppers with my head lowered for action
and my cart sailing along. I made it into the check-out line and
was in the middle of congratulating myself when I looked at
the woman in line ahead of me and saw THE mother and her
small boys. By now there was a line of people behind me, so
there was no place to go. I mumbled something to myself about
"Why should I fight it?" when someone tapped me quite
sharply on the right shoulder and said, "Pay attention." Since,
visibly, no one was at my right shoulder, and I knew I hadn't
made it up, I figured that it just might have been the Lord or a
visiting angel who had spoken.

Once when I was telling this story to several hundred
women, a woman at the close of the meeting asked, "Does God
really tap you on the shoulder and say, 'Pay attention'?"

I answered, "Well, no. Actually sometimes He says,
'*Sweetie*, pay attention.'" I wasn't trying to be irreverent or
flip. It simply is true that if you and the Lord are on speaking
terms and doing as Paul says, "praying without ceasing," there
is bound to be a running dialogue between you and the Lord.
So you find the grocery store is not too different from whatever
spot you choose for your private devotions.

I must say that only a few rare times have I "heard" an audible
voice in my prayer life. More often than not it's like having a
fleeting thought cross through my mind. I always wonder if that's
a "Joyce" thought or a "God" thought, but the trick here is just to
pay attention to what's happening around you and be ready for
action—just in case it's *not* a "Joyce" thought.

Actually though, at that moment in the store I really wasn't
too sure exactly what I was supposed to watch for because
about the time I decided to pay attention, the store sort of blew
up all around me. And after that I didn't have any trouble

giving the situation my full, undivided attention.

It seems the littlest boy in the cart ahead of me had run out of wonderful things to do, so he reached up, grabbed the gum and candy rack, and gave it a healthy yank towards him.

As it toppled over, it connected its wires with another rack, a large one filled with a jillion candy bars. The two racks toppled together, spraying the front of the store with all kinds of gum, Lifesavers, cough drops, and giant Peter Paul Almond Joy bars.

One sixteenth of a second later, his mother, the volcano I mentioned earlier, erupted into a hot, molten mass of hysterical screaming. All of which was directed, of course, at her two little boys.

Everyone was immediately called on duty for a "red alert." Coming over the store's intercom was a deep urgent voice calling, "Code four ... Code four", and box boys, managers and produce people came running from every direction and up every aisle to the front disaster zone. Personnel who had unwisely chosen to eat their supper in the back room were "volunteered" into duty, and no one was spared the job of helping to clean up the mess.

Manager, assistants, meat men, clerks and box boys flew into a flurry of action. Kids were stuffing all kinds of candy into their pockets. Only a few were stopped by customers as they raced for the outer doors. Women were rolling their carts over piles of Rolaids. Men were softly crushing candy bars to death under their shoes, and my feet and ankles were lost in a sea of Lifesavers and Dentyne gum!

By now the volcano in front of me was pouring a screaming hot torrent of big words, dirty words, and threatening words into the four little ears below her. Apparently, she didn't think she was getting through to them so she reached down, grabbed one boy by his sweater collar, the other by his neck or one shoulder, swooped them up to her eye level, and then really let them have it!

She shook those boys until I was sure blood would come gushing out of any convenient opening, and she let them and everyone else in the store know that they were to *"shut up and not move!"* After one more violent shake for emphasis, she slammed them down on the floor.

They froze in ramrod positions. I thought they'd stopped breathing.

Bedlam was still taking place all around us, so she started helping the pick-up crew. I was moving slowly out of shock and beginning to help too, when, out of the corner of my eye, I saw a disturbing thing take place. The littlest boy *MOVED*.

I was horrified. He was deliberately disobeying his mother, and I wondered what could make him take such a dangerous action.

To avoid his mother's eyes, he moved backward in a slow cautious motion toward her large straw purse. Then with deliberate but smooth movements he reached behind him into the purse and from its depths he inched out a small, faded blue blanket. All the time he was slowly pulling it out of her purse he never took his eyes off his mother.

Finally, when he had his blanket safely tucked under his chin and was sure it was in the right place, his tense little shoulders relaxed, he breathed quite a loud sigh, and color returned to his face. Tranquillity, as I have rarely seen it, erased the fear from his eyes, and as he began to sway from side to side he ever so gently hummed a little tune. I was completely captivated by his serene little face and this tranquil scenario.

It was as is if the Lord broke through my thoughts and softly whispered, "Here's the down-to-earth lesson I want you to learn. When this little boy's whole world quite literally crashed down around him, when *everything* was wrong, and his very life seemed threatened, he did not reach for his nervous, tense, screaming mother, but for his only help ... his 'gentler' ... his faded, blue blanket, and he was comforted by its presence."

I stood there thinking. This faded blue blanket probably never had given him a moment of pain ... never given his teeth a rattling ... never given his ears a screaming or threatening lecture. In fact, the only time there was any trouble was when he had temporarily lost it to the washing machine and didn't find it until later when it came out of the dryer. But there in the store, the blanket had been sought, found, and used ... and the shattered pieces of his whole little world clicked silently back into place.

I'm quite sure the check-out girl or a box boy named Jim never knew, as I came through the line, that I was getting a glimpse of being a woman of God in a new dimension. On the spot I promised the Lord I'd learn all I could about being gentle. I'd let the Holy Spirit take this "sanguine" to school to learn gentleness. I decided that while I had thought gentleness was beyond me, I'd now do everything, with God's help, to be my family's "gentler." I didn't want to leave that work to some synthetic blue blanket, and I thanked God for the gift of gentleness that I hoped He was about to help me attain.

I left Alpha Beta that day with a willingness to *earn* a repuation for gentleness. It felt like an opportunity to grow, and I was fascinated by the change of attitude I'd experienced in just a little over an hour.

Just this past year, I went back to this scene with the little boy and his faded blue blanket ... and because it is years later and I'm in a very different place, mentally, physically and spiritually (hopefully I've matured some), I saw this wonderful incident in a new light. I recorded my present views in a book called *My Blue Blanket* and decided that the images of the little boy and his blue blanket bore retelling. It's like taking down a book from your shelf and finding your underlined passage from a long ago reading, and then seeing something unmarked that's in the next sentence and finding yet another gem of a thought.

But back to the gentleness factor I observed with the little boy and his blanket.

Since gentleness was not (and at times still isn't) a natural grace in my life, the first thing I tried was to think of the gentle women I knew. I came up with two or three.

One was the very first of my wonderful secretaries, Sheila. But holding her up as an example didn't do too much for me because just by her personality Sheila seems to have been born with a gentle and quiet spirit. I never heard her raise her voice above a soft Jacqueline Kennedy whisper. (I'm convinced she trained and guided her two little children by hidden remote control buttons as does my sister Marilyn. It's fantastic! So, I scrapped *that* idea.

Finally, after I'd tried, to no avail, to manufacture some methods of achieving gentleness, I did what I should have done in the first place. I went back to the Lord. Fortunately, He had waited for me to catch up with Him.

In my prayer time it seemed to me that God had to back me up a bit, for He pointed out that for me gentleness would have to begin in front of my washer. My washer?

Yes, because the first person, after me, that gentleness would affect in my house was my daughter Laurie. Slowly it began to dawn on me that when Laurie put her blue jeans in with a white wash, added nylon knit lingerie and washed the whole load on the hot water cycle, as she was prone to do, I *then* had a giant opportunity to *think* and *practice* kindness and gentleness. But somehow, standing in front of my washer and just looking at what I thought was a very messed up wash load was not conducive to acting out gentleness.

The whole New Testament is filled with directions for being kind to each other (I Thess. 2:7, 2 Tim. 2:24, Jas. 3:17 to name a few). Does this mean only to strangers or casual acquaintances? Not in this lifetime. We must start by being kind and gentle to our *own* family. Yet, how could I be kind and gentle to a daughter who insisted on ruining so many of my wash loads? Once she went through a "break-cycle" during which she dropped bowls and destroyed nearly every glass I had in the house. It's funny now that she's all grown up how these laundry loads and broken things are absolutely of no consequence. But, at the time, they were such a big deal to me!

I bring this up only to say that I'm fairly sure the beginning of gentleness with others starts by remembering some of the unexplainable and rather dumb things I did when I was a little girl.

My mother's pretty blue cotton dress, for instance, comes to mind. I was fascinated by how quickly Clorox bleach put white polka dots on that navy blue dress when I sprinkled it on. Or, there's the day I was sick with the flu (and quite bored) lying on my Grandma Uzon's couch. In order to amuse myself I took a razor blade and sliced open all the seams and cording around the cushions on the couch. It was all so entertaining until the next day when my grandmother lifted up a piece of cording and said, *Vat is das?* I was seven years old at the time. From the way Grandma yelled at me that day I thought I'd never get to see my eighth birthday. In fact, my grandmother, till the day she died, never missed an opportunity to shake her finger at me, make threatening sounding remarks in Hungarian and point to the nearest couch so I wouldn't miss the message. My list could go on.

I found I could become gentle with Laurie and her incredible way of messing up a load of laundry if I remembered that for most of my childhood crimes I *was* disciplined, but it was rarely done out of raw anger. When my mother spanked me, it was by no means a heavy, uncontrollable swing in the dark; it was explained calmly and yes, even gently and then *firmly* applied to my "seat of knowledge." Even in her spank I could sense a controlled type of gentleness and that, combined with my sense of knowing I deserved it, made it almost acceptable. At least I didn't feel my mother was being unfair. I would have liked to have avoided all confrontations about my behavior, but Mother did things in such a gentle way that had she not chastised me in some manner I would have missed the healing experience of being forgiven.

About eleven million times (well it *felt* like that) I had to go through the this-is-how-we-do-the-wash-Laurie-Honey routine, but I began employing the technique of kindness and gentleness. And I believe it paid off, and not just for Laurie but for me as well. It was accomplished not only by remembering my pledge of gentleness and my childish mistakes, but by recalling the beatitude that says, "Happy are the merciful, for they will have mercy shown to them" (Matt. 5:7, Phillips' translation).

I found that I had a whole closet full of gentleness, mercy, and kindness when I took time to remember some of the moments when mercy was shown to me!

Colleen Evans says, "All of us, until we go to be with Christ, will have 'blackouts' in our lives in one area or another." I must remember the times of mercy when I *did not* deserve them ... when my blackout times were really bad, yet someone was tender and gentle toward me. The mistakes, sins, indiscretions, or even plain thoughtless acts of others have been at some time or another my very mistake, my indiscretion and my thoughtlessness. How dare I forget the gentleness of others and the Lord's? I must make allowances for others as I have been given consideration in the past; I must temper my reaction with gentleness, remembering someone's gentleness with me.

There is great merit in the Oriental custom of "saving face." Far too often we are quick to call a spade a spade, set something immediately right, or instantly correct a situation. Sometimes when we do that to someone we push the person into a corner with absolutely no way to "save face." We wonder then why others are so defensive. When we hit hard without a thought for gentleness or kindness, the other person has no choice but to come out swinging, ready for a fight.

The beatitude about being merciful is a beautiful promise, but it is not without its conditions. *If* I am merciful, I will have mercy shown to me ... seems to be its message.

The day I began to learn gentleness I realized how important it was to help Laurie save face. So I took some of the heat out of the conversation by saying, "This is probably *my* fault because I've failed in really teaching and training you to do the laundry. Maybe I wasn't clear enough in my wishes as to when and how to launder. So for that I take the responsibility and the blame."

At this point, instead of her usual lip, Laurie did not become hostile or defensive. She just stared meekly at the washer. I then explained how terribly frustrated I was becoming over the ridiculous wash loads she was running. I don't think it stunts our children's emotional growth to learn that their mother and father have a few hang-ups of their own. How else are our children going to know we are real people with real problems?

What actually was said was not nearly as important as the fact that somehow I was able, with a dose of gentleness and mercy, to discuss a very annoying problem. I went through the wash instructions a number of times after that, and I was rather sure that before she got married and settled down to do her own laundry I'd probably go through the routine again. And I did. But from that time onward I found I didn't regard this "explaining time" as a chore or distasteful duty. It was just something that, as a mother, I was going to have to do. I dropped the phrase, "Laurie, how many *more* times am I doing to have to tell you how to do the wash?" It helped me to think gently ... "This is my darling Laurie, I'm going to count this as another opportunity to train her in the routine art of laundering."

Now that she and Terry are married and have two children, I notice she handles the large daily loads of wash *quite* well, thank you very much. Ah ...thank the Lord, I must have done *something* right.

However, it was years of learning about wisdom, kindness, mercy, and gentleness, and Laurie occasionally tossing her jeans into my all-white Clorox wash, before either of us made it through the laundry issue.

Not long after I decided to spend some funds from the Gentleness Account, I wondered how the Lord would let me show gentleness to my son, Rick.

In the nineteen sixties the cultural pressures around us had most of us believing that after a boy reached the age of four you didn't turn him into a sissy by kissing or hugging him. Most touching was rather taboo. It was loudly touted that you taught a little boy to be a *man* by being hard as nails and steeling yourself to show no emotion (like his father and his grand-father before him). You let him know that it was not manly to be touched or moved emotionally over a good book, play, or movie and, Lord forbid, if he should be so moved over something that he cried ... it was believed that you should step right up and inform him that "real men don't cry." Our society looked on a man's tears as a definite sign of weakness, of being overly sentimental. The implied conclusion was that if a male of our species cried, he certainly wasn't much of a *man*. Actually the idea that real men don't cry (or eat quiche) started almost a hundred years ago in the Victorian age when men were supposed to be strong, and women weak and fragile.

My son Rick's generation of young people introduced the so-called hippie movement. Kids who revolted against their upbringing and dropped out of mainstream society. Kids who decided they would set up their own value system. They would be different from their parents and from the establishment. So the hippie generation spent a great deal of time touching, sharing food, drugs, diseases, and beds. And yes, they said it was all right to laugh and to cry together.

I believe now, looking back, I can sure understand their reactions and responses to life that drove them to express verbally and physically the gamut of their emotions and their need to reach out to one another and to be touched.

With my own children, I made a quiet but concerted effort not only to touch and kiss Rick and Laurie but to tell them, out loud, not just by slipping them some extra money, (although like my mother did for me, I did slip them money occasionally) that they were loved.

It was never easy, but I endeavored to give the kids my *time*. I felt if Rick was to be a gentle-man-husband-father-adult he'd have to see gentleness in action at home.

The opportunity presented itself clearly one afternoon when Rick came home from school. He was obviously distraught. Since I'd become aware of the art of gentleness, I'd learned to slow down my typical motherly pounce when I sensed trouble in my kids. So I waited a bit until I couldn't stand it and then managed the quietly probing question, "Something wrong?"

His answer, "Oh, Mom," just heaved out. Rick continued, I've just seen an awful thing ... the guy who sits next to me in drama class had taken acid [LSD] between class periods and when we were twenty minutes into our class this guy went absolutely berserk ... his face, his eyes, everything were so horrible."

He went on for a few more minutes describing the distressing events, how they happened and how it took him and three other guys to get the kid out of class and into a friend's van.

Rick was emotionally spent, having witnessed so close at hand someone completely out of his head because of a bad drug trip. It wasn't a moment for a lecture on drugs, a moral or theological diatribe of mine; it was simply the right time for gentleness. So, without a word, I crossed the kitchen floor to where Rick stood, put my arms around his six foot frame and held him close for many minutes. Silently I prayed for Rick and for the unnamed boy working his way through a bad drug trip.

That time of gentleness in the kitchen must have soothed Rick's troubled mind beyond what I hoped or guessed for because after a few minutes he straightened up, looked down at me and said, "Mom, when I was a baby I probably needed to be held ... but *never* more than just now." I left the kitchen with my face awash with tears. I had almost *not* gone over to him because of all that brainwashing about letting a grown boy heal his own wounds. I also walked away from the experience wondering *who* would gentle him if his mother or father did not? What teacher, friend, or neighbor would gentle his grieved mind? What type of *blue blanket* would he turn to if he failed to find it at home? Where would he have gone had I not responded to God's leading? The responsibility to be a gentle woman was and is awesome!

Those experiences with Rick and Laurie were lovely training sessions in how the richest lady in town should spend some of her great wealth. They were also the preliminary training grounds for on-going lessons about gentleness for me, as a woman.

In my thirty-plus years of dialoguing with people, particularly women, I've asked a lot of questions. By that I mean I've asked hundreds of times, "How's your heart?" Most always the response I've received has not been a medical report, but "feeling" words about the emotional health of someone's heart. And usually the answer is about a relationship.

The oft quoted line, "No man is an island", comes to mind ... only I'd phrase it, "Nobody is an island." We all have relationships, whether we love them or hate them, or whether they are great or not so great. It's a fact of life. A part of being alive. And it's of interest to me that for all the many times I've asked about someone's heart, besides telling me about a relationship, they usually, in their own way and from their own perspective, talk about the presence of gentleness or the absence of gentleness in that relationship. We seem to attach great significance to the act of being gentle to others and to our own need of it ... whether or not we call it gentleness, or admit our need of it.

As a woman, I am beginning to understand better my own need for the healing process of gentling between myself and my loved ones. More and more I'm aware of how vital gentling is in our ability to withstand and endure the daily traumatic experiences that assail us.

Perhaps in the past I haven't taken the need for the gentling process in my life and the lives of loved ones seriously enough. But as I grow older I'm taking another, maybe even a more in-depth, look at it now.

All any of us have to do is watch the evening local and national news to see that the world at home and abroad has gone irresponsibly mad. One night last year our TV news informed our community that in beautiful Austin, Texas, insanity had struck again. While two teenage girls waited for their best friends to finish their work and close up the "I Can't Believe It's Yogurt" shop, someone or a group of individuals came in and murdered all four girls. Then, presumably to cover up their crime, the killers took whatever they were after, left the bodies of the four girls where they were, and set the shop on fire. The perpetrators of this horrific crime are still at large almost a year later. I keep asking myself, how can such devastating and heinous crimes be committed and what kind of person would do such things?

I wonder, has there ever been a time when our battered and bruised emotions or our minds needed the comfort of gentling more than now. I doubt it. There is enough violence, enough abuse and enough growing madness in our homes, on our streets, in our land and in the world today to make our need for gentling each other one of our highest priorities.

The word *gentle*, as a verb in one of my dictionaries, defines the act of being gentle like this ... to be gentle is "to raise one from a vulgar condition."

When I think of the grieving parents (two of the four girls were sisters), the families and friends of those teenage girls whose lives were so hideously obliterated, I know I've no power to change the circumstances; but here in the quiet calm of my home, right now, I can gentle them a bit through my prayers. And if I knew them personally, I could go to them and at least gentle them with my quiet hugs. I believe all of us have the ability to do something about raising others from the "vulgar" conditions of their lives.

In fact, I believe there's never been a more appropriate time for gentling one another. Men and women need to gentle each other. Husbands and wives need to gentle each other. Mothers and fathers need to gentle each other. Parents and children need to gentle each other. Adults and children need to gentle each other. Teachers and students need to gentle each other. Professionals and their clients or patients need to gentle each other. Relatives and neighbors need to gentle each other. Management and labor need to gentle each other. Government and people need to gentle each other. "A utopia" you say, "Not in this lifetime!" Perhaps ... but to gentle others simply means being kind, tender, and giving comfort. It also means being merciful, thoughtful, and yes, even humane. Which is all, incidentally, very scripturally correct behavior for any who call themselves Christian.

The Old and the New Testaments talk both of God's anger and of his gentleness,

Thou hast given me the shield of thy salvation; Thy right hand sustains me. Thy

gentleness has made me great.

(Psalm 18:35 Modern Language)

Later in the New Testament Paul picks up the same theme by writing about the "gentleness of Christ" (II Corinthians 10:1, *King James*). Then the apostle admonishes us as servants of the Lord to "be gentle unto all men" (II Timothy 2:24, *King James*).

And Paul goes on to explain in Galatians that one of the fruits of the Spirit listed right along side of love, joy and peace is *gentleness* (Galatians 5:22, *King James*). And there are many more scriptural references about God's gentleness toward us and our gentleness to and from others.

We must keep in mind that gentleness is not a harsh noisy syncopated drum beat in our lives ... No, it's more like a beautiful flowing melody, softly sustained by drawing a bow across a violin string. It's an on-going song ... caring, soothing and comforting, reaching into the deepest part of our souls.

Recently I had a speaking engagement in Seattle, Washington. So I took advantage of the opportunity and went a week early to California to spend Thanksgiving with my children and grandchildren.

Very early one morning, after I'd put in quite a restless toss-and-turn night, I decided to try to sleep in instead of helping to get my grandchildren off to school.

I was sleeping so soundly that I missed any noise my grand-daughter Jennifer may have made getting up and dressing, even though we were sharing her bedroom. I was still deeply asleep, lying on my stomach, when someone touched me.

Slowly I awakened and realized that I'd been very lightly and gently kissed on the back of my head. It had been such a soft brush against my hair that it took me several seconds to respond. But as I raised up and turned my head, I was just in time to see the back of my eleven year old grandson James, all ready for school, backpack and all, carefully tippee-toeing out the bedroom door.

He had said nothing, but James had communicated his love for me ever so tenderly; and the gentleness of the moment will always catch in my heart like it does now.

Gentleness breathes life and health into all of our lives especially in these times of stressful living when we find our hearts and minds strained almost beyond their endurance levels. We would be fools to ignore the treasures contained in the gentleness account.

One more memory, an older one, comes to mind. It happened when I was about seven years old and the Barnum and Bailey circus came to Owen Sound, Ontario where my dad was the pastor for the First Assembly of God Church.

I begged my mother to let me go with Bobby and Betty, my friends who lived below us on the second floor of our flat, to watch the unloading of animals in the railroad freight yards. Reluctantly Mother let me go, but she gave me a firm warning to "be back in two hours."

Of course it was all so interesting that Betty, Bob and I lost any and all concept of time. And only as we were running home did we notice it was almost dark and that we'd been gone many hours.

When I breathlessly bounded through the front door I was stopped short as I saw my mother kneeling beside our living room couch. She had been praying, and when she turned to look at me I could see her eyes were red from all the crying she had done, but I could also see that on her face was written the word *relief*. All she said at that moment was, "Oh Joyce-

Honey", but I knew later I was going to get it. It was obvious that Mother had been absolutely positive that I'd been hurt, lost, kidnapped, or all of the above.

I'll never forget what happened. Even though she was obviously happy to see me, I'd given her an awful scare, and she gave me a spanking to impress me with the fact that I'd disobeyed. It *did* the trick. I was definitely impressed. But what I remembered most from that experience was what happened immediately following the spanking after I was sent to my room. There, while I was sobbing alone, Mother came in. She patted and dried my face, took me into her arms and, without a word, nestled me down on her lap. After quietly holding me for a little bit she explained once more why it had been wrong for me to break her rules. She was mercifully brief. Then carefully she comforted and gentled me with her hugging arms and her words of how she loved me and how precious I was to her. I never loved her more.

In Isaiah God tells His people, "I will comfort you there as a little one is comforted by its mother" (Isaiah 66:13, *Living Bible*).

My mother has been gone a long time now and of course I'm too grown up to climb on her lap to be comforted and gentled; yet this beautiful passage in Isaiah is a treasure house of gentleness that God has given to all of us. More than once, as a woman, a wife, a mother, a mother-in-law, a grandmother, and a stepmother, I've needed to be gentled, and God has done it not only through my family but directly, as well.

Jesus Himself, our great pace-setter for right now, said, "Wear my yoke—for it fits perfectly—and let me teach you; for I am gentle and humble, and you shall find rest for your souls; for I give you only light burdens" (Matt. 11:29, 30, *Living Bible*).

In reality I think this gentleness account has barely been dipped into by most of us. There are still huge reserves for us to use. We still have a lot of living to do in Christ, and we're still growing and learning. So I'm excited about this account and all its possibilities.

LOOKING BACK

Now that Laurie is no longer a teenager but in her middle thirties with her husband Terry and two children, I've had a chance to watch her as she handles running her busy household. And wouldn't you know, she does everything in her home and with her family just beautifully, including the wash loads. Surprise?

Back last Thanksgiving when I was with them in California I had to wonder what my impatience with Laurie as a laundering teenager had been all about.

I was helping Laurie to clean and cook, etc. for the big Thanksgiving dinner she and Terry were giving. In the midst of some pretty serious hustle and bustle she and I had this brief exchange. I called to her from one of the bathrooms,

"Laurie, I'm finished in here now, what shall I do?"

"Mom, just do the wash."

I hesitated for a second and then said,

"Oh, but Honey, I don't know how you like it done."

Laurie yelled above the roar of her vacuum cleaner in the living room, "Mom, just do it ... after all, you're the one who taught me all I ever wanted to know about laundry."

I smiled and was looking for her box of soap when Laurie suddenly rushed into the laundry hallway and with a very concerned look on her face said gently, "Mom, Terry just said that I was cold and harsh to you ... he said I should apologize ... Did I hurt your feelings?"

I hugged her and told her I wasn't hurt and there was no need to apologize. (I'd been so busy trying to figure out the combinations on her washing machine dials that I hadn't given her response a second thought.) Relieved that we were all right, Laurie pointed out the box of soap (right in front of me) and went back to her vacuuming.

It was bread cast on the water coming back to me. For Laurie, afraid that she may have been too curt with me, had come in to me and used her own account of gentleness and mercy. As I did her wash that November day it was clear I'd been given a dose of my own teachings. Laurie had "gentled" me, and I smiled with the memory of how significant our early days together had been. My own impatience with Laurie could have always stood like a wall between us. How grateful I am for the gentleness and mercy account which quietly pushed beyond some of those tempestuous teenage barriers.

HEART OF THE MATTER

Our own personalities (or attitudes) may lean significantly towards our being highly impatient human beings. Mine sure does. Maybe impatience comes in our genes? I don't know. Whatever.

But when I put impatience up against gentleness and mercy ... I feel quite certain that for most of us gentleness does not come from within us (like it seems to from Sheila or my sister Marilyn), but rather it's a trait we decide to reach out and take. A trait we deliberately *choose* to develop and employ in our daily lives. A conscious act of our will.

We may not completely achieve the exchange of impatience for gentleness. But I believe, if we *want to*, we'll see the riches of blessings that choosing gentleness and mercy can put into our accounts ... and the enormous dividends they will produce.

FOUR

The Opportunity Account

Usually when we are on the lowest rung of the economic ladder, the only thing we believe will help us is to climb as many rungs as possible in the shortest amount of time. We think, "If only I had some money—or some *more* money."

Newspaper columns and TV programs on money management, investments, etc. are abundant. With all of this storehouse of information available to us, you'd think we'd all be wealthy. But nothing is that incredibly simple.

I was born in 1932, and since that year followed 1929, '30 and '31 you all know what kind of baby I was. However, my mother never got around to calling those times "depression years"; they were always "opportunity years." I rarely heard *anyone* call the depression an opportunity.

She saw the three dollars a week Dad was making in his little church, not as the meager sum it was, but as a giant opportunity to trust God. If she longed for wealth, she didn't nag or complain to Dad about it.

Apparently, though a few men in our congregation made (a whopping) nine dollars a week, my mother was aware and sensitive to others who made even less than my dad's three dollars. I know from later conversations with her that Mother's prayer life covered the financial needs of people in their church, family, friends, and neighbors, as well as our own. I also know that when she held our own dire straits up to the Lord, she fully trusted Him to take care of us.

The strange and wonderful thing, then and even now, is that when we ask God to meet our needs ... He really does. It may not be in the way we expected. It may not be in the dollar amount we hoped, but, somehow (and sometimes barely in the nick of time) God provides exactly what we need.

My mother was pretty extraordinary. She didn't whine or pine for the clothes or the furniture she couldn't have. She took what she had at hand and expected the Lord to make her extremely creative. And so He did, many times beyond her expectations or ours.

Whoever said, "Necessity is the mother of invention," never knew my mother, but if he had, he definitely would have dedicated that saying to her.

The hardship of being poor in the early thirties, at least for me and my parents, seemed to force to the surface of our lives one rich dividend after another.

In fact, I didn't know we were poor until I was graduating from high school and then I found out only by accident. By that time my father was dean of men at Southern California Bible College when they were still located in Pasadena, California. Dad's salary included: Board—which was student dining room institutional food; Room—which were three tiny rooms packed into the end of the boys' dorm; and a salary of $150 a month. I had no idea we had so little.

My Hungarian mother would bring that bland dining hall food into our rooms, whisper lovingly to it, add a bit of onion, sour cream or whatever, and make it taste absolutely delicious. Necessity and poverty made her an excellent cook. She'd collect broken, unused furniture no one else wanted; then she'd fix, paint, antique, and lovingly coax it into delightful tables, chairs and couches. She found that an old beat-up cotton rug purchased at the

Goodwill store could be cut down, washed, and dyed a bright color. I remember that we had fancy "area rugs" long before interior decorators ever invented them.

I also remember her reputation for creativity on the campus. Students were always dropping in on Mrs. Miller to see "what she's done now."

I never dreamed that taking one's poverty in stride, using it to really trust the Lord, and expecting Him to help you be extremely practical and creative was not the normal, everyday thing all Christian women did. And I never suspected until I was much older that I lived with a woman who was extraordinarily rich and who planted the seeds in my heart of taking what I had, thanking God for it, and turning it into something of value.

James has a verse which describes Mother very well: "God has chosen poor people to be rich in faith" (2:5, *Living Bible*). I began to recognize her great storehouse of wealth about three weeks before my high school graduation.

I was seventeen and graduating from Pasadena City College which at that time was a four-year institution. There were the last two years of high school and the first two years of college. Each year the two graduating classes had one pageant-like graduation in the famous Rose Bowl. Twelfth graders (that was me) on one side all dressed in white formals with the fourteenth graders on the other side dressed in the traditional cap and gown.

Mother showed no sign of hysteria or shock when I said that I would have to have a long, white formal for graduation, even though at the moment she had no idea where we'd get one. She had me take her shopping the next day, and we went to all the fancy stores, including Bullocks. I had more fun because she made me try on one lovely dress after another. Of course, we didn't buy any because, as she explained to the salesclerks, "We're just looking and getting a feel for what we want."

The dress that really took my breath away and produced a lot of oohing and ahhing from my mother was a beautiful white organdy. It had a hand-tucked bodice that was embroidered all over with tiny white seed pearls, and a full skirt with tucks all the way to the floor. Mother, after her heart had told her *"this is the one,"* said quite casually as she turned the tag over and read the price, "Oh, that's what Daddy makes in a month."

I was stunned "A *month*?" A hundred and fifty dollars? The price of this dress is what Daddy makes a month? It was my first clue that we were poor. We were next to welfare and I hadn't even suspected it!

At school all the next day, I pondered about my poverty-stricken state and dreamed of that unobtainable white dress. I could easily visualize my graduation night. All the twelfth grade girls in beautiful white gowns, and me, in the middle of them, resplendent in my white sweatshirt and grubby black skirt. After school I mulled over the problem all the way home on the bus, but was nowhere near ready for the scene that would spread out before me when I walked into our living room.

My mother, who by her own admission was not a seamstress, was sitting at her beat-up sewing machine and merrily stitching away. Flowing from her fingers was a long, white organdy, full skirt. It was tucked every six inches to the bottom. And lying over on our dining room table, all put together, was the tucked bodice. It took only a glance to see where I'd sew two bottles of tiny seed pearls. I was so carried away with the dress, Mother's happy chatter, and visions of graduation night in the Rose Bowl, that I forgot to ask where the white organdy had come from.

I slipped off my school clothes and was in the middle of my fitting session when I noticed the marvelous quality of the organdy, and my mind did a mental double take. I blurted out, "Where did you get this beautiful stuff?" She didn't drive so she probably didn't go to town and buy it—besides all that yardage would have cost a fortune.

Mother took the pins out of her mouth, smiled, shrugged her shoulders, and said, "Oh, it's just some material I had here." She went right on pinning the tucks as if to say, "Hey, no big deal."

I thought, *Some material she had here?* and then the momentous truth dawned on me.

"Mother," I was almost yelling, "this organdy material was the beautiful crisscrossed curtains we *used* to have in those windows right there!"

"Mmmm, yes." She went on, never missing a pin or a stitch. Now I *really* understood the facts:

1. We were poor.
2. It didn't matter.
3. I had an extraordinarily gifted mother!

Without even wincing, my mother had cut up her treasured organdy curtains. No regrets, no martyr complex, no "poor me," no lecture on how long she had saved to buy them on sale; just this mental process, "Let's see, I need a long white formal for Joyce ... (Ah, yes, the full crisscrossed organdy curtains. They'll do nicely." Snip, snip.

The dress hung in my closet for years, and now it's in a Chinese cedar chest my parents gave me for my sixteenth birthday (instead of a car). It's a wonderful reminder of what treasures being poor *can* bring. It also makes me smile when I remember the seating arrangement of graduation night, because I sat between two of the wealthiest girls in all of Pasadena's social register. Each of them spent much of that night telling me how fantastic my dress was. "A little something my mother whipped up," I kept saying. And in my heart I kept repeating, "My mother ... what a woman!"

We are continually being told today how awful it is not to have *everything*. Besides newspaper and magazine articles, we also have television hammering home its golden message of BUY, BUY, BUY!

Each commercial tells us that if we have this product we will be either

1. happy
2. satisfied

3. beautiful
4. smart

or all four. This kind of advertising, over a long period of time, leads us to believe that we must *have* everything offered for sale or our lives will be terribly incomplete. So we have developed a "wish" mentality to buy and accumulate things at insane levels. What we often don't see is that "things" which bring us great material wealth may also deprive us of the opportunity to trust God, so we don't get to see Him provide in powerful, exciting ways which are beyond our expectations.

This kind of materialistic thinking puts fantastic limits on God, and I feel that's one of our biggest mistakes. We miss so much. I know now that what made my childhood an incredible adventure was the fact that my parents never really knew *how* God was going to act, only that He *would*.

Just before I was born, during the time when my dad received only three dollar a week from his small church, my parents had an experience which they told and re-told. It was one of those times when they were down to their last fifty cents in the whole world.

My folks had spent the morning discussing the food they needed and just how they'd spend the last remaining fifty cents. Mother got carried away and imagined how good bacon sounded and tomato juice and pineapple and so on. Before too long she had an unrealistic list of twenty-one items. Dad advised her that even in the depression, fifty cents wasn't going to go that far.

Later, as Dad drove to the store to buy just some essentials, one tire decided not to cooperate, breathed out its final breath, and went flat. The nice man at the service station said he could install a new boot so the tire would last a few more months and that it would only cost, uh huh ... fifty cents.

Once when my Dad recalled that day for me he vividly described his discouragement and how he drove slowly home and tried to figure out how he'd tell the news to Mother. After he got home and since their shopping plans had been canceled, they decided upon the only thing they knew to do. They had a prayer meeting. Not a sad prayer meeting but, as much as they could make it, a joyous one. It was a prayer meeting between two people who were in love with the Lord and each other. They thanked God for all the things they had. When they quickly ran out of that, they thanked Him for the gift of His life to them. Before they got up from their knees they sang together the Doxology ..."Praise God from whom all blessings flow ..." Almost forty years later my father's eyes glistened with tears as he recalled how tenderly they had sung that day.

Their singing under those circumstances was done in joyful obedience and was wonderfully Christ-like; maybe that's why God was so spectacular to them in the following moments.

After their praying and singing, mother went into the kitchen and was stunned with surprise. Calling out to Dad she told him that there were two large bags of groceries on the table. Together they eagerly began unloading the cans and boxes of food. Their amazement blossomed into reverent awe as they realized that not only did they have the essential food items they had prayed for, but every item my mother had so whimsically wanted as well. The bacon, tomato juice, pineapple ... they were all there. Many more than twenty-one items. They had no idea who was responsible for their bountiful supply except that God had heard their prayers. Then, again, they sang the Doxology, this time at the top of their voices!

Over a year later a couple was visiting in Dad's church. At the end of the service the man talked about how good it was to come back to visit since they had moved to another town the year before. Then, casually, he said, "By the way, a year ago—before we moved—I got sick on my job and asked if I could go home. The boss let me, but by the time I reached home I was fine and I decided to return to work. Then my wife, who was standing out in the driveway, said, 'I know *why* you're home ... Reverend Miller needs some groceries. As long as you're home let's go get them some food.'

"So, we went to the store. My wife went down one aisle and I took the other until we had all the items. Somehow we *knew* which ones to pick. Then, when we got to your back door we heard you praying and singing. We didn't want to bother you, so we crept in quietly, set the groceries on the kitchen table and left. You did get them, didn't you?"

In retelling the story my Dad would just shake his head and smiling he'd say, "We never knew how God was going to work ... He just did."

All through their lives my parents watched God work His miracles.

In one of my mother's many notebooks I found something that really summed up her attitude toward financial matters.

"In life you strive and reach out for gold.

In heaven you walk on it!"

In poverty she had been truly blessed and as I grew up she passed those blessings on to me.

We had no money for concerts, going abroad for study, or learning the fine arts, but she never let that hinder a cultural education she had mapped out for me.

When I was six and seven years old we lived in Michigan. Mother and I took long streetcar rides from Highland Park to downtown Detroit. We spent wonderful hours looking, listening, and learning in the Detroit Institute of Arts Museum. One part of the museum I'll *never* forget was the Egyptian section. Mother never got to travel to the Holy Land even though she reminded the Lord of it many times. The next best thing was taking me to the Egyptian section and seeing mummies and all the biblical artifacts. Long after those days, when I was in Cairo, Egypt researching for my novel *Joseph*, the Cairo Museum brought back a flood of rich memories. And to this day I never see anything about the Holy Land without remembering those happy times of learning.

Poverty taught her to develop the art of observing. Traveling across Detroit on a streetcar with her was quite a fun-filled adventure basically because we didn't just ride the streetcar.

She'd make up wonderful games which forced me to see all there was to see. I had to look and to watch so I'd be aware of everything that was going on around us on those rides.

Now that I look back on my own kids' childhoods, I remember the happy times of riding the San Francisco cable cars, trying to teach and train them to see all that there was to see like my mother had done for me. I received the ability to observe and perceive because back in Detroit my parents were too poor to own a car. I have a rich inheritance because of our lack of material things.

The stories of how God met my parent's needs were told to me and were repeated to my children. How my parents trusted the Lord, and how He provided not only food, clothing, and money, but some of the most profound lessons in living and the great art of persevering in faith.

Aside from reliving and enjoying these stories of God's provisions in my family's past, I never really opened my own Opportunity Account until it was thrust upon me. Inappropriately, I thought at the time.

Our children were still small and finances were a constant hassle. My husband managed a toy store in Pomona at the time, when out of the blue, he was offered the opportunity to be the CEO of a large department store. Overnight, it seemed, he went from managing twenty or thirty employees (at peak Christmas time) to a store with some sixty to seventy employees. The mental transition was rough, but we didn't care as we were sure God had opened this door in a most unexpected way. I praised the Lord for this new, challenging job and we were sure that He was in this move. Especially since the new position provided a larger salary.

My husband hadn't really cared for the retail business, but his education was all in business administration, and so he never considered anything but retail (or wholesale) selling as a life's occupation. He had worked hard and done well in every job he held from the time he was a box boy in his teens through this point in his life. He felt good about the position.

But less than three months after we "knew" God had given us this advancement, I was startled at lunch time to see Dick driving up our driveway. He came in carrying personal articles from his desk in one hand and a two weeks' severance paycheck in the other.

"I was called into the main store and *fired* this afternoon," he explained in a stunned tone of voice. He had taken his role of breadwinner with utmost conscientiousness and to be fired was an experience he never thought he'd have.

I'll never forget that afternoon or evening. As the reality began to settle in we cried, prayed, talked, rehashed this whole venture, read the Scriptures and didn't come up with one single clue as to why this had happened. Nor what the future would hold for us.

Some time during that afternoon I had some pretty dark thoughts. At one point I heard Satan's snappy little voice crack, "So, now you call yourselves Christians and look what happens! God told you to quit the toy store and take this one, didn't He? See how God *loves* you? How *He* rewards you? How will you live? How will you pay the bills? What will you do? Jobs are scarce. How will you keep a roof over your heads or feed your children?" I was very frightened. Nor could I remember all the stories I'd heard about God providing for our needs.

The afternoon came to an ironic climax. At 6:30 p.m. we were scheduled to go to a church dinner for about thirty couples, where I was to be the speaker. The topic I had been asked to address was, "How God Leads Us in a Christian Marriage."

I had planned to use a number of illustrations which demonstrated God's leading, but I scrapped the talk. I had a microscopic amount of willingness to go to that dinner. However, we went (reluctantly) and a funny thing happened to me just as I was about to speak before those couples.

The Lord seemed to say to me, "All afternoon you've both talked and have listened to each other. Later you listened to your dark thoughts, but now, Sweetie, you listen to me!"

I could do nothing less than stand before this group of older, wiser adults, open my mouth, and beg the Holy Spirit to speak to me *and* my audience. To my incredible amazement I heard myself tracing the Lord's hand in our lives up to the present time. Then, because I didn't want to burst into tears I didn't share that my husband had been fired that day. I simply told them we were experiencing the greatest challenge and the greatest opportunity of our lives. I related that it was, to date, the most contradictory time of our lives, *yet we were going to trust the Lord anyway.* God would supply our needs, and, before I ended, I could see the Lord had already touched our own hearts.

As we left the meeting, nothing in our circumstances had changed or lightened up in the least. But flooding my soul was the same "knowing" my parents had experienced. That incredible presence of God and that inexplainable peace and assurance that everything would be alright.

Struggling through the next few months of bills and unemployment, I dipped into the Opportunity Account with a heavy hand. I learned 250 ways to be creative with one pound of hamburger. I began to teach myself how to sew. (No easy trick for someone who got D's in Home Ec.) I made drapes for Rick's room, fancy French valances and curtains for Laurie's room, braided rugs, sewed all Laurie's and my clothes (not with Vogue patterns—they're written in Portuguese—but with Simplicity Jiffy), and managed all that on a $12 treadle sewing machine I found at an auction. Since I *never* had the desire or the patience to sew even a straight seam before, this turned out to be one of the most fascinating, exciting times of my life.

I did find though, that in the beginning I could only sew for a maximum of ten minutes. I've increased that time, but not by much. However, I remember praying over that sewing machine, being frustrated by a difficult collar or sleeve, and hearing the Lord answer, "Leave this sewing machine and go do the dishes." I did. Then later, when I returned to sew the collar or sleeve, the pattern instructions seemed to make more sense and the material just zipped into place without a whimper.

Dick was still without work many months later when someone suggested he take an aptitude test to see what kind of work he'd be best suited to do. He did, and when the results came back they indicated that he might do particularly well in financial matters. This caused him to recall that in retail management he had liked the financial side best. So my prayers included requests about a job involving finances. Then, again, out of the blue (and God's hand) he had lunch with a mortgage broker from our church and came home with a job. In a brief span of time he became the vice president of this small but active loan company. Now I was convinced that being fired was in God's plans all along. My husband had been too conscientious to leave the retail field just because it was tough or he didn't like it. It had taken an out-and-out firing to move him. And that was precisely how God acted.

About this time I mentally and smugly phased out my Opportunity Account. I thought I didn't need it as our financial situation was getting quite secure; then the whole bottom dropped out of the mortgage loan business in California. My husband and hundreds of loan officers just like him were out of work with no place to go. In great haste I reopened the Opportunity Account and asked the Lord to overlook my foolishness. This time, however, there were no tears, only a little panic, and just a small period of dark thoughts and Satan-inspired depression. I quietly laid out our financial problems on the table and said, "Uh, You see this mess, Lord?" He must have, for the Lord's peace was so strong I was like a little girl giddy with joy. That must be what James meant when he said, "Consider yourselves happy indeed ... with trials of every sort" (1:2, Knox's translation). In the natural it was ridiculous to be at such peace when everything was still quivering, yet that's exactly how God works.

My husband reminded me, rather matter-of-factly, that it was entirely possible that we'd lose our home, cars, and maybe our furniture, and then he asked me to adjust and try to plan accordingly.

Being strictly female, my immediate response was that I could probably lose the cars without too big an adjustment and maybe the house, but the furniture? I didn't think so. I wasn't feeling too peaceful or happy all of a sudden. (Have you noticed how one's spiritual level has a tendency to go up and down like a yo-yo?)

However, it was at this point that sanity returned and the Opportunity Account came into mind reminding me of its availability. Of course, I wasn't about to call a joyous singing prayer meeting as my parents had, but I did go to the Lord with these words, "Father, if we lose the house and cars, that's really all right. However dear Lord, about the *furniture*, You know I shopped, fixed, mended, upholstered, painted, or antiqued nearly every piece? I'm terribly fond of those chests, tables, and chairs. Help?" It seemed in those moments I heard these thoughts in answer, "If you lose every stick of furniture in the whole house, Joyce, what have you lost ... really? You and your loved ones are still my children." The unruffled quiet words stung their way home to me. I've never been too keen on having my security ruined or even threatened, and somehow my furniture had become extremely dear and precious to me—without my realizing it. The beatitude says, "Happy are those who claim nothing, for the whole earth will belong to them" (Matt. 5:5, Phillips' translation). The beauty of those words broke over me. It was silly of me to be so terribly concerned and to be so connected (glued) to those tables and chairs even if I did practically make them.

So, I went to my husband and said, "I've been praying and thinking about all this and here's what I think ... if we lose everything, what have we really lost? Pieces of wood, fabrics, glass, motors, material things but nothing more. We may have to live in a tent and (perish the thought) camp out for years, but so what? We still have our life, we have Rick and Laurie, and more important than that, we have Christ—*living in us.*

I began daily to thank God for the lay-off and watched for his magnificent hand to begin working. Many months later my husband was offered a starting trainee position in a bank. Our financial crisis eased, and our losses were light. The lesson was marvelous for me because I knew we could have lost everything. Many people have. Yet the experience taught me the value of *always* keeping alert for the "Opportunity Account" moments. I was able to see that I could survive, in fact, as James said, I was even able to *rejoice* in my troubles, because they added to my growth and storehouse of riches.

In the following years, God allowed me to accumulate some earthly things and I learned to enjoy them without their owning and controlling me. For instance, at one point my living room had elegant white carpeting, pale blue chairs, and blue-and-white print couches, which all blended into a restful, peaceful room. Besides teaching me how to make something out of nothing, the Opportunity Account and my mother showed me how to take a small treasure and turn it into a large beauty. My blue-and-white living room and the rooms I've had since all seemed to reflect these lessons.

But there is one thing I'd like to make very clear about these *possessions.* If I lost my entire home and all its lovely things, its pictures, accessories, my piano, and my lovely rugs, my world would not collapse and neither would I. Truthfully, I'm sure I'd miss those lovely, rather irreplaceable things, but they are not my whole world. I know now that my trust and faith are not in them and they do not own me. I do not really own them either. They are a generous loan to me from the Lord.

I am afraid it's only too true that when we put all our attention and importance onto furniture, houses, and other possessions, and then lose them all ... we are stunned with the losses and can't find our way as people who could otherwise be strong and recover from such devastation.

Perhaps we do the same thing in regard to possessing

people. We say things like, "I'd die if anything happened to my husband." Or, "If my son was killed in war or murdered, I don't know how I'd exist." But the truth is, God gives us people and things and they are really on loan to us. We can enjoy husband, children, furniture and home. We can love them for what they really are—*gifts!* But it is possible to spend a whole lifetime possessing people and things and miss the joy of understanding how to *trust* the Lord and use the Opportunity Account.

If God entrusts money or possessions to our care, remember, it is what we *do* with our wealth that really counts, and whether it runs us or we run it. The scriptures tell us to be good stewards of our money. Let's thank Him constantly for the money and possessions we do have and seek his Holy Spirit for direction as to how to spend and enjoy it.

On the other hand, if we have nothing and we live in a real measure of poverty (I don't think I, as an American woman know a whole lot about being poor compared to many women of the world), then we need to use our lack of worldly possessions to make us rich in faith. My mother did, and it not only made her wealthy in the faith but also in a hundred creative and practical ways she never suspected. Even if we are homeless by anyone's standards but have learned to thank God and have responded to this unique challenge, any of us can be the richest lady in our town.

In one of her endless notebooks, my mother wrote: "If God is going to do something wonderful ... He starts with a problem. If God is going to do something spectacular ... He starts with an impossibility."

My family is still learning about the dividends of being poor. A few years after my mother died, my sister, Marilyn, then twenty, got a chance to study in Israel one summer. When she first told me about this incredible opportunity to go to the Holy Land and, at the same time, earn ten units of college credit, we were simply jubilant over even the thought of it. But the amount of money Marilyn would need to have came to over fifteen hundred dollars; and as far as we were concerned, it could have been fifteen million. Yet we trusted and reasoned that if the Lord wanted her to go to Israel, He'd supply the money. I desperately wished I had been enormously wealthy and could foot the whole bill. Yet, that might have deprived us of a rich blessing—using the Opportunity Account. It also would have put God in a remote position and we may not have seen Him in action quite so vividly! We "prayed in" most of her flight and expense money and secured a five hundred dollar loan. Just two days before she was to leave, the Lord worked through Clare and Conn Bauer who gave her the last of the fifteen hundred dollars she needed. Marilyn went off to Israel praising God! I stayed home doing the same thing!

Once there, Marilyn discovered that she was very short of extra spending money, even for emergencies or miscellaneous needs. She'd worked all the previous school year, and, with the help of some scholarships, had barely made it through school financially. So "extra" money was non-existent. Yet in Israel she was to fully discover the Opportunity Account. When her only pair of sandals fell apart she prayed over their tattered remains, told the Lord about her needs, and *thanked* Him that her only pair of sandals had fallen apart.

The next day an American woman, studying at the same Institute, found Marilyn and said, "Honey, God has laid it on my heart to buy you some sandals." It was as simple as that. All summer long God provided just enough money from different sources and in beautiful ways, even though at one point Marilyn and her roommate, Barbara, had all their money stolen.

By the end of her summer training, Marilyn counted out what money she had left. She knew she would need money for food in Rome on the trip home. She found she had enough for the four days in Rome since her hotel and flight were prepaid. However, the Opportunity Account was unexpectedly put into her prayer life when the day before she was to leave Israel, she was told she needed an extra ten pounds for something called an exit tax.

Without telling anyone, not even her roommate, that she was short ten pounds, she breathed to God, "Lord, You know in order for me to leave Israel tomorrow You have to pay the exit tax. Ten pounds. I don't have it. Now I thank You that I *don't* have this extra money." And with that she left it in God's lap. She was her mother's daughter and was well into the Opportunity Account.

That same day Marilyn finished classes and exams, and checked her mail box to see if she'd received any mail from home. The box was empty. She was disappointed but not panicked and so, again, she told no one of her need.

Late that same night she felt she ought to check her mail box one more time. When she reached the mail room and peered through the glass in her box she could see that there was some paper all folded up. Instantly she knew it wasn't ten pounds but she smiled when she saw her name scribbled on top of the paper. All summer she had put little happy faces, notes, poems, etc. in most everyone's box at the school and she was just sure someone was sending her a fun note or poem.

However, when she opened the sheet of paper an English ten pound note fluttered down to the floor. For a moment she stood very still just looking at the money. Then slowly she opened up the paper and read,

To Marilyn,
Love, Jesus

To this day she does not know the name of the human heart God used to work this spectacular "impossibility," but that was a summer Marilyn never forgot. It was a first-hand experience at watching God put the Opportunity Account into action.

Marilyn is like my mother—not very wealthy in the material things of this world, but astoundingly rich in faith. Remember, none of us would *ever* be really rich in faith *without our times of poverty.*

A friend, Dick Walstrom, had the chance to open up this

account, as I discovered by his Christmas letter. Like you, I get my share of Christmas letters each year, but this one was extra special. It was a typically long, newsy letter, interesting only to dear friends, but I'd like to share some parts of it here. He wrote:

This past year has been one of the most discouraging for our family. Two days before last Christmas I was laid off from work and was out of work for almost four months. I just couldn't find work anywhere. We were not prepared financially for this disaster. But with God's help and guidance and assistance from relatives and friends, we have withstood the strain. We give God all the praise, because without our faith in Him, we would have given up and almost lost everything.

We did have to sell our trailer, which upset our kids, but they understood what we were going through.

In April I started work as a salesman. My neighbor was quite instrumental in getting me the job. I never sold anything in my lifetime, so I was scared on my first day. But with God's help I learned very quickly. At the end of each month I would generally end up in the top fifteen salesmen out of thirty-five men—you must agree, I couldn't have done it without His help.

We're so grateful for our kids and our family life!"

Then, after a personal rundown on his children, he ended by saying,

I know this is a much more serious letter than usual—but we want others who have faced these problems, or those who might have to face them in the future—to have faith in God. He will give you direction— if you believe in Him.

And of course last, but most important, is my wonderful wife, Connie. Without her strength and love, I would have given up a long time ago. During troubled times—if a family isn't pulling together— complete failure would set in! But God strengthened our love for Him as well as our love for each other. Our love for each other is stronger now than ever before.

In closing, if the Lord can provide a Jewish man (my neighbor) to help a Christian (me) to get a job—then He can perform miracles for you!

As I finished the Walstrom's Christmas letter, I understood clearly that I had read the writings of a very wealthy man. He had his perspectives and goals in the right order. He and his wife had learned that the first secret of adjusting and accepting problems was to be found in rejoicing in them. Their growth was obvious. Over the years I've watched these dear people as they enriched their lives through their Opportunity Account.

Not too many months after I received my friend's letter I read 2 Corinthians 4 from *The Living Bible* and thought once more, very vividly, of this friend and countless others (me included) who walk daily by faith. Paul described his life and the lives of his co-workers in this manner,

We are pressed on every side by troubles, but not crushed and broken. We are perplexed because we don't know why things happen as they do, but we don't give up and quit. We are hunted down, but God never abandons us. We get knocked down, but we get up again and keep going ... These troubles and sufferings of ours are, after all, quite small and won't last very long. Yet this short time of distress will result in God's richest blessing upon us forever and ever. So we do not look at what we can see right now, the troubles all around us, but we look forward to the joys in heaven which we have not yet seen. The troubles will soon be over, but the joys to come will last forever (vv. 8, 9, 17, 18).

The Opportunity Account is a huge asset and readily available to us as Christians. Perhaps this is the moment for you to discover its remarkable potential in your life.

LOOKING BACK

During the time I was going through my unworld divorce settlement I had just the right set of circumstances to see if my faith and beliefs about the Opportunity Account were really valid. Or not.

My losses included my home, job, office and over half of all the furnishings I'd made, collected or purchased.

However, those losses, in view of today's perilous economy are not unusual. Bankruptcy, Chapter Eleven, homelessness, starvation, and nouveau poverty are realities for millions of people all over the world.

But I'm always caught off guard (though you'd think by now I'd know better) how at every turn, with every loss and with every painful event God surprises me with his unusual, unexpected and quite spectacular methods of filling the needs of my life, from the large and overwhelming to the tiniest and most fragile.

HEART OF THE MATTER

The Opportunity Account is available to us all, but it cannot operate if we do not choose to develop and use it.

Thanking God for what we have and do not have requires a decision of our wills to act. Amazingly ... God takes it from there. For He knows when our losses and need of things are massive, and He keeps the account standing ready, marked: OPEN.

FIVE

The Resource Account

It was Clare Bauer, my dear friend, who bounced into my living room, barely said hello, and fired off at me, "Okay, so you're writing a new book. Is it about your mother?"

My round-about answer was, "Well, no, it isn't, but yes, in a way it is."

"You've got to write about her. *That's* the book I'm waiting for," she said almost indignantly.

"I am, I am," I countered, "but I'm not writing her whole life's story. I'm just making her a part of the book in various chapters."

Clare didn't look too pleased and I had to smile. There she sat asking me to write about a woman she'd never laid eyes on. My mother died before Clare had even met me, yet Clare was asking—no, really pleading with me to write about my mother.

"Please write about her. From what you and Marilyn have told me I know others need to hear about this remarkable woman," Clare said, restating her feelings.

My mother was indeed a remarkable woman. She influenced us and hundreds of other people in fantastic ways, even after her death.

My brother Cliff's wife, Bonita, once said to my sister, Marilyn, "There's one woman I really want to be like. That's your mother."

77

"But, Marilyn questioned, you've never met her. She died before you even knew Cliff."

"Yes, I know," Bonita said, "but everyone who ever did know her talks about her, and they never mention what she *looked* like.

They simply talk on and on about her personality and her relationship with God. She must have been a real woman of God, and I want to be just like her."

Breast cancer took everything from my mother, Marion Uzon Miller, except the sparkling spirit that fairly danced out of her dark brown eyes. In less than three years after her mastectomy and halfway through her fifty-seventh year, the Lord said, "That is *absolutely* all the pain I will allow her to bear." Then, much like James W. Johnson's poem-sermon of *Go Down Death*, God issued the command for Death to bring Marion to Him.

She went more than willingly, but I let her go with halting reluctance. We had her dressed in her favorite flowered voile dress (the last one she and I bought together), surrounded her with a huge garden of flowers, and packed in Dad's church with hundreds of people who listened to her funeral service.

John Gustafson's tenor voice rang out in her favorite songs "Until Then" and "My Heavenly Father Watches Over Me"; Chuck Leviton read a poem he had composed about her, "Marion Miller, the Quiet Fanatic"; Dr. Ted Cole, my pastor at the First Baptist Church in Pomona, California, preached a stirring message about her life ending with "She is *not* dead." When it was ended we all stood and sang "Great Is Thy Faithfulness" and watched as so many dear and precious people filed past us. We said our good-bys and tearfully ached with pain as the casket lid was closed upon her.

Even though she was a brilliant Bible teacher, she was never nationally known or famous nor was she published. So it should have been the end of her; but then I found all her notebooks: big spiral ones, little spiral ones, date books, secretary pads, loose-leaf binders, and even the diary she kept when she was in her early twenties before she met my father. They were a treasure house of ideas, a cache of theories, and a reservoir of inspiration. The very essence of fifty-seven years of being God's woman.

Once when my mother was being introduced to speak for a large group of women, the mistress of ceremonies referred to Marion Miller as a "real, live saint of God."

I was sitting next to her, so I leaned over and penciled in on the top of her notes, "Hey, how about that, you're a real, live *saint* of God!"

Her deep brown eyes really came alive, and she took my pencil out of my hand and wrote on the margin of my Bible, "Look out when anyone calls you a saint. It's a funny thing about saints—God usually calls them home!"

She would not like me to write of her as some sanctimoniously, pious woman, an unearthly holy saint, for she was nothing like that. She was real. A live woman with a husband, three children, and two grandchildren. With brilliance she taught four Bible classes each week. With compassion and sensitivity she taught Christian release time with children each week. With vision and a mission she worked at everything in Dad's church from refinishing all the pews in the main sanctuary to being Sunday school superintendent and DVBS coordinator each summer. With great wisdom she was the spiritual advisor for the Christian sorority Dale Evans founded called, Lambda Theta Chi. And toward the end of her life she suffered the real, agonizing pain that only cancer is capable of inflicting.

She was *no* saint, but she lived her fantastic life one moment at a time. It seems to me that what gave her that invisible aura was that she managed her life with an extraordinary running dialogue with her best friend, Jesus. And *that prayer life* really did set her apart!

She was so connected with the Lord that after listening a while she knew the exact moment to look into the eyes of a child, teenager, young adult, or senior citizen and whisper, "Oh Honey, there's someone you need to meet. He's my dearest friend. Let me introduce you to Him." Then calling the person by his or her name she'd lovingly coax them into the presence of the Lord.

As I was reading a great little book, *Witness Is Withness* (Moody Press, 1971) I thought of my mother's unique ability to share the love and joy of Christ with just about anyone. I think the author of that book, David Augsburger, would have loved my mother because she lived out his subtitle, "More showing than telling."

The last year of Mother's life, in spite of enormous pain, she introduced many people to the Lord. It was impossible to keep track of all of them. In fact, her counseling ministry was so heavy in her last year that in order for me to talk with her I had to go to her home, pick her up, and take her shopping.

Once when I arrived to pick her up she put her finger to her mouth, shushed me up, and hustled me off down the hall into the den. As I passed the living room I glimpsed a tense, drawn young woman perched on the edge of the living room couch as I went flying by. Some two hours later, after I'd read a couple of books, I heard the front door open and close, and then my mother came in. She was just radiant.

"Okay, Joyce-Honey, we can go now," she said cheerily. I could barely hear what she was saying because my attention was riveted on a small, pearl-handled revolver she was holding in her hand.

"Oh, that," she casually tossed off ... "Well, the young lady in the living room came early this morning. She was determined to use this on herself if she didn't find any answers. We've prayed and talked and God really came through. I introduced her to my friend Jesus ... and when she left she said she didn't need this anymore."

I probably was the only shopper walking around the May Company hours later that day with her mouth hanging open.

Her work with the PTA was equally amazing. I don't know how they did it, but a PTA board made up of mostly Jewish women elected my mother, the Gentile wife of the local Community Church minister, to be their Spiritual-Inspiration Chairman year after year, long after her kids were graduated! But it was not without a minor problem in the beginning.

The first Christmas she served on the board, she was instructed by the board to refrain from talking about Christmas. Of course she talked that over with the Lord and then stood before the board with her reasoning. She made the observation that Christmas was not merely a Gentile holiday but a national one as well, and that she really felt that it would be unpatriotic to ignore it. However, she impressed their socks off when they found she had boned up on many Jewish traditions and she said she was fully qualified to speak on both Christmas and Hanukkah. Which she did. In fact, her presentation to a packed auditorium was so marvelous the local rabbi asked to meet her. He called her a "storehouse of information," this Marion Miller, wife of a minister, and said she could speak in his synagogue at any time.

Year after year the PTA called her back to serve. She never compromised her Christian testimony, but at the same time the Lord wisely led her into a ministry of inspiring hundreds of Jewish women about their special Hebrew heritage. Many of them quietly accepted their Messiah.

We got a glimpse into what mother must have meant to these women just hours after she died. The PTA president pressed a large, bulging envelope into my Dad's hands and said, "Reverend Miller, no one asked for this or started it; was just a spontaneous act. When we found out about Marion's death this morning, PTA women started coming to my house. They all gave me money. There's several hundred dollars here. We are unanimous, Reverend Miller, we don't want it spent on flowers. Please give it in memory of Marion to your church to carry on its work."

Hundreds of tributes were made to my mother in the days and weeks after her death, but this one was particularly touching.

As I said, my mother had a running conversation with the Lord throughout her life. Her prayer life was certainly her most remarkable and memorable trait. She had a sense of wonder that helped her to be very creative. Adding to that was a sense of humor that seemed to help her to never take herself too seriously. But it was definitely her prayer life that set her apart from others.

No one was left out of her prayers. Immediate family, distant relatives, church members, PTA women, sorority women, children, teenagers, Bible class women, neighbors-*everyone* was lovingly and lavishly prayed over.

I was particularly rich in that much of her praying was for my brother, sister, and me, and one of the things I miss most, now that she's gone, is this aspect of her life which so encompassed all of us.

Mother phoned me almost every morning of the last five years of her life. She'd wake me up with the words, "Good morning, Joyce-Honey! Well, tell me, what wonderful thing has God done for you today?" She'd really get to me ... especially since I am not nor ever was a morning person.

"Oh, brother!" I'd groan. "Mother, I am not even fully awake yet and you want to know *what exactly* has God done?" And because she was always so sure God *had* done something, I was always pushed into finding *something*, anything to praise the Lord about.

After she had made the usual noises mothers make to daughters, she'd tell me what she was praying about that morning or (better yet) something the Lord had taught her, and she'd come up with one pearl of great price after another.

Two months before she died she phoned and after the usual opening of "What's God done for you," she rather earnestly restated the question.

"Now, Joyce," she said seriously. What *has* the Lord done? I just know He's really done something terrific!" She was as excited as I was blasé because I couldn't think of *anything* the Lord had done, much less something terrific.

"Now, I mean it" she repeated, "what's happened today?"

"Nothing, mother, absolutely nothing."

"Did you get anything wonderful in the mail? Are you going to do some TV work? Is your radio broadcast syndicated?"

"Mother," I said chuckling, "all I got in the mail yesterday and today were four bills and one rather negative letter from a radio listener of mine who thought I said, 'creme de menthe liqueur' when I really said, 'This recipe takes creme-de-menthe-flavored sherbet.' And, unfortunately, the answer to all those other questions is *no*.

She could barely believe me. "Are you positive?"

By now I was ready for some explanations, so finally she said, "Well, early this morning I couldn't sleep so I began praying for you and the Lord rather clearly told me He was going to open up a brand new ministry for you. Something you've never done before and something that will reach thousands of people."

I laughed and said, "Well, God's not going to do anything today, Sweetie!" She ignored my flippancy and wouldn't let me dissuade her from what she *knew*. She insisted that the Lord was working out a new plan for me.

"You mark my words, dear daughter, on this day, the fifteenth of July, 1966, the Lord has opened a new ministry in your life!"

We talked some more and I remember ending our phone conversation by teasing her about how clouded her crystal ball was. Stubbornly she refused to believe that "nothing" had happened.

Two weeks later, while I was at Biola University taping several weeks of my "Here's Joyce" radio programs, one of the secretaries handed me a large box of mail from listeners. Right on top was a letter from Floyd Thatcher who was then director of publications for Zondervan Publishing House.

As I read it I was absolutely sure it was some kind of a joke. I held it out to Ginger, my secretary, and said, "Hey, does this sound like it's a serious offer?"

She read it and said, "It sure does. He's read your *King's Business* magazine articles and it looks like he wants you to consider writing a full-length manuscript—a book!"

I was stunned and could hardly believe it. Zondervan was a world-famous Christian publishing company and they were

asking *me* to write a book. It was too much. I wouldn't even
have written a column for *King's Business* in the first place if Al
Sanders, the managing editor, hadn't asked me what I thought
of the magazine. When I complained that it had no women
writers or editors and no womens' page, Al responded with,
"Fine, *you* write it!"

Coming home from the radio taping that day I was surprised to find my parents had decided to drive across Los
Angeles for a visit with me. My mother was gray with cancer,
but when the usual hugging and kissing was over I said, "Oh,
Mother, you're not going to believe this, I've *got* to read you
something!" And I dug the Zondervan letter out of the box.

Cancer had begun to whip her into its own form, so I sat
down on the edge of the couch where she was lying and read
Mr. Thatcher's letter. When I finished I said, "Well, what do
you think of that, Mother? They want me to write for them. Did
you ever think your daughter would write a book?"

I still see her so clearly in my mind's eye. She was too weak
to even lift her head up, so she just laid there, smiled, and said
very gently, "I *always* knew." Then softly and with just a touch
of smugness she added, "I thing if you check the date on that
letter, you'll probably find it's marked July 15."

And it was.

God shared His thoughts, His plans, and His ideas with her.
He revealed Himself to her in His Word as I've rarely seen
before or since.

Perhaps then you can imagine since I always had this kind
of praying mother, how utterly shocked and dismayed I was
when after her death I found the heading, "When God Did Not
Answer My Prayer" in one of her notebooks.

They were almost the words of a heretic. She who believed God
could do anything had suggested He did not, or could not—I
wasn't sure. Eagerly I read on.

Before you start reading her story, stop right here. Now, try to
remember when you asked God for something and He didn't

answer you. Or, ask yourself when was the last time you said either to yourself, God, or someone else, "I've prayed but God doesn't answer my prayers." Remember? Good. Now go on.

Mother wrote:

"*The time:* early fall of 1931. I was pregnant with Joyce.

"*Place:* Oil fields of Michigan. In the home of the Pastor of the church.

"*Why:* Three weeks of evangelistic meetings.

"*Needs:* Personal ones and this was during the time of the depression.

"*Outward appearance:* I had one yellow and blue silk shan-tung two-piece dress. I got that before we were married. I did buy for my honeymoon a sample hat made of striped silk ribbon marked down from $8.00 to $4.00. I owned a white wool coat. (I bought that too before marriage.)

"*Amount received per week:* $7.50 (It took us $10.00 to get there.)

"*Situation:* While there for those weeks we lived with the pastor, shared his home, food, and hospitality. The frying pan was ready each morning from the day before. Potatoes were always fried in it. The coffee pot had grounds of yesterday's coffee and another spoonful of new coffee thrown in each morning. They just let it boil. The eggs swam in the grease. For lunch we had fried potatoes and beans from the same greasy pan. Stewed tomatoes, and coffee from the same pot from breakfast. Supper was fried potatoes and beans again (from the same pan). Tomatoes, coffee, and, for variation, fried bacon with flour sprinkled on it.

"Clifford and I coasted into Oil Fields, Michigan on our last gallon of gas, and before too many days we wanted to get out if for nothing other than to change our menu for just one meal. We waited each night after the service to see if we'd get an offering, but found that no offering would be given until a love offering was taken at the end of our three weeks. We had to wait three weeks! Eternity seemed shorter.

"Usually the mail would bring us a dollar or two but each

time the mail came it was just mail—no dollars. I prayed for just *one* dollar so we could go out and change our diet.

"Each morning, after the mail arrived, we would have prayer with the pastor and his wife. When the pastor received mail with any money in it, he would waive the money high above his head to the Lord and have a praise service. Then he led in what he called a 'Jericho March,' to thank God. We all stomped around his living room and around their dining room table in sort of a sanctified dance line.

"But there was never any money in our mail. I went into the bedroom early one morning and petitioned Jesus to please send us just one dollar—just enough to get us to the nearest restaurant for a hamburger. (You could do this on a dollar in those days.) A real joy swept over me and I got up from my knees confident that my petitions were heard and that the answer was on the way! I encouraged my husband. He, by now, had the making of several good-sized boils, but I assured him that God would send us mail on the morrow.

"He did! But when we opened our mail, there was no money. My heart sank. Then God spoke and told me that He *would* give me the one dollar. The pastor, about that moment, opened his mail, sent up a shout, and waved a $10 bill. As plain as your voice, God spoke to me and said, 'He will give you 10 percent of his money as an offering.' So I, too, got in the hallelujah line and thanked Him for my dollar. But after the Jericho March I groaned as I saw the pastor put the $10 back in his envelope. I never saw it or my dollar nor was there any mention of it—ever.

"I felt depressed and quite uncertain as to my assurance, His Word, and answered prayer. So I thought, *Well, maybe I'd better pray for a two-cent postage stamp so I can write my mother and ask her for a dollar.*

"I went into the bedroom again and prayed in earnest for God to give me the desire of my heart and send me just one two-cent stamp. Again I had complete assurance that my prayer was answered.

"The next morning after our reliable fried potatoes breakfast we had devotions and then opened the mail.

"We got mail—but no stamps. But bless me! Pastor got happy, started his Jericho March and waved a *whole page* of two-cent stamps. You will get ten of those two-cent stamps,' the Lord whispered to me. I joined in the praise march for I *knew* I was getting *ten* stamps instead of the one I'd asked for!

"But in horror I watched the pastor as he put the stamps back in the envelope without a word.

"This time I was really bewildered, confused, and doubts raced through my mind. I doubted particularly the power of prayer and made up my mind that it must not be God who was assuring me. I'd never get a tenth of that ten dollars or the ten stamps—after all it was just all in my mind!

"Finally our three weeks were over and we left with our love offering and my husband's boils.

"*Later:* Times were hard, money scarce but we settled in Saginaw, Michigan, and there we received our training of wants and needs. Joyce was born, but as times were hard my heart grew harder. *I knew it didn't pay to pray*—even if I did, God didn't hear or care or even know my needs—let alone supply them!

"My weight dropped down to 89 pounds. I doubted God; I hated people for being selfish; I lived in bitterness within and hardship without. Joyce, our baby, was sick and needed nourishment. It was a desperate time.

"Two years later, my husband was called to assist a pastor in Dearborn, Michigan, for one week. To supply his own church in Saginaw, he invited an evangelist to fill his pulpit. He had them stay in our home for that week.

"It happened that one day after I had gone through a form of prayer and family worship, a discussion began about God's answers to prayer.

"I felt I had to let the fountains of the deep break open in my heart, and I poured out my experiences in Oil Fields, Michigan to the evangelist's wife. I told her I could never feel I would ever be assured of answered prayer again.

"I thought the tears that fell down her cheeks were in pity for me, but not so—she had a story to tell me. She and her husband had just come from two weeks of meetings with that very pastor. Our names had been mentioned. The pastor in Oil Fields had spit out these words, 'The Millers are proud people and very rich. Why she had silk dresses, a hat, and a beautiful white coat. He had a good car and do you know, we were poor, yet *we* had to feed them, and they never offered to buy a thing for the table? They were stuck up and fancy! Why, once I got money through the mail and I thought, *I'll share one dollar as a tithe with them*, but then I thought, *No, why should I? They have more than we do!* Then, a day or so later I even thought I'd give them ten stamps from the page I got in the mail, but then I thought, *They should give me stamps, not I; they are selfish and better off then I!*' I listened and was just stunned.

"What really hit me as I listened to this woman was that God *had* heard my prayer! He *had* spoken to the pastor, the instrument that was to give the answer. But the individual heard the voice of God saying, 'Share ten percent of your blessings with the Millers,' and a big 'No!' was sent right back to God. 'Give ten stamps to the Millers,' God commands.

"'Why should I?' He counters. 'They're better off than I!'

"God spoke to my heart through this experience. God answers prayers through *you* and *me*. He does not drop dollars from the sky like rain, nor hang stamps on the trees like fruit—this is contrary to His laws. You fulfill and answer His prayers by being touched and moved to give to God's work and God's children.

"I promised God that day that when I pray and no answer comes, after self-examination and being sure of no hindering sin, my prayer will be, "Dear Jesus, *thank* You, Lord, for *hearing* my prayer. I know it's not You who fails—I'll wait till another hears Your voice and answers Your will and commands."

My mother learned this lesson well, early in her marriage, and prayer became her most beautiful contribution to those who knew her and to many who never knew she prayed for them.

All through her life, from that time on, Mother responded to even the faintest suggestion from the Holy Spirit. She never wanted to be guilty of failing to be God's instrument in answering someone's prayer, like the pastor in Oil Fields, Michigan.

I remember many times she visited someone, and that visit marked the turning point in their lives. Or, she would write someone a letter at the precise moment they needed it. And Mother was just as generous with her money as with her time.

In the last year of her life, she had a little fund started in an envelope for a pair of white summer shoes. She'd been thinking about a pair of white pumps for just months. One Sunday when she had amassed five dollars in her little envelope and as she walked into church, she heard the Lord saying, "Give those five dollars to Bill over there."

She hesitated for a second and, then cheerfully muttering something about, "Okay, Lord, so there go my shoes," she went over to the young man and gave him the five dollars. Later we learned that her simple act of kindness was the turning point for a financially desperate young man. He needed the five dollars to enroll in a special course in night school, and to think that God would answer his prayer for five dollars was utterly incredible to him. Bill's faith in God would never again drop so low because of Mother's pressing those five dollars into his hand.

The next morning Mother opened her mail and the Lord said, "Now, Marion, about those shoes you wanted"—and out of a letter from a friend fell ten dollars. Her friend had written, "I just wanted you to have this!"

After some thirty years of trusting and praying she wrote, "Christians today, as always, are waiting on God to answer their prayers. Many have waited long and have doubted God has heard. Others have become offended especially when God has said, 'No' (or worse yet, 'Not now') and they have charged

God foolishly. When Job's whole life went out the window the Scripture says, 'In all this Job did not sin or charge God with wrong' (Job 1:22, *RSV*).

"God's waiting room is the most tiresome and unpleasant place in our Christian experience. We do not like delays or denials, for hasn't God said, 'Ask, and it shall be given you' (Matt. 7:7)? God has reasons for delays. Some He will reveal to us, others we may never know, but one thing we know for certain—God *never* makes a mistake!"

I cannot write about this unique and lovely mother of mine without using the word *faith*. In her writings *prayer* and *faith* are so enmeshed that you hardly find one without the other.

Mother wrote: "God has established the law of prayer and faith. Prayer is being conscious of need—while faith supplies it.

"Prayer never obtains anything from God unless faith is present and active. Faith never receives anything from God unless prayer makes a petition. Prayer and faith work harmoniously together—both are necessary in their distinct function, but they are quite different in their nature.

"Prayer is the voice of the soul, while faith is the hand. It is only through prayer that the soul can establish communion with the Creator, and it is only through faith that spiritual victories are won. Prayer knocks at the door of grace, while faith opens it. Prayer makes a petition, while faith presses through the multitude to touch the hem of His garment and receive from His giving hand. Prayer quotes the promises, while faith boldly proclaims the fulfillment of the promise!"

Mother lived her almost sixty years on prayer and faith. This Resource Account is mine because of her great examples lived out before my eyes.

My mother was wealthy beyond words. An heir of God! I found one paragraph that sums her up completely. This is her personal testimony, her statement of faith, in her own words.

"When God found me, I was no better than a cobblestone—

hardly worth picking up. But He took me into His laboratory of grace, and by the chemistry of atoning blood, He processed me, and I came out as His jewel—a bit rough, I'll admit, but after a few years of cutting, buffing, and polishing, He will present me at last before His throne, and I shall be absolutely flawless. Miraculous though it be, it is true that God, through the power of the Cross, can transform you into a precious jewel.

"What a joy it is to go through life knowing that we are among heaven's gems and 'In That Day' when He makes up His jewels—we shall be included!"

Mother prayed when she felt like it, when she didn't feel like it, when it was easy, and when it was hard. She prayed when she cooked supper, when she gardened, (several times neighbors caught her talking to her roses), when she vacuumed, while she read, and as she listened to thousands of people pour out their hearts to her.

She was not some religious nut who went around mumbling to herself all the time—she simply talked to God as easily as she breathed. When you talked with her you knew *He* was listening in too.

Every time I meet people who are really on speaking terms with God as my mother was, I am not surprised to find that, like my mother, their time spent in praying and studying God's Word is *always* a cherished part of their lives.

My mother knew how to pray as some people play the piano, *by ear*. I am always amused when someone asks me to *show* them how I play by ear. It's impossible—try as I may I can't explain how I have *always* been able to hear a song once and then play it.

It was the same with Mother and her praying. Once when I heard a series of messages on prayer by Dr. Curtis Mitchell, Professor of Bible at Biola University, I was amazed at the similarity of his views on prayer (which he had developed after a considerable study of the prayers of Jesus and the disciples) to my mother's views.

He captured the essence of mother's prayer life when he spoke about the act of prayer. He said, "Prayer is an act of specific requests." Jesus was always specific in what He prayed for. Dr. Mitchell went on to tell that in his own prayer life the more *unconcerned* he was, the more general his prayers. When he was deeply *concerned*, his prayers were completely specific. That was my mother's secret in her prayer life—very specific requests!

She was so concerned—honestly, sincerely concerned for people, things, and even rose bushes that looked a little puny—that she always prayed *specifically*. She gave God every opportunity to answer specifically, and *He did!*

One other interesting pattern in mother's specific prayer life was that she petitioned God for *material* needs about 10 percent of the time, but 90 percent of the time was for the *spiritual* needs of herself, her family, or a friend or acquaintance. At many of the prayer meetings I've been in the percentage was completely reversed—90 percent asking God for material help or physical help and only 10 percent asking for spiritual needs.

We all have this Resource Account available to us. It is not just some extraordinary gift God *only* gave to my mother. Her only edge was that many times she had no place to go, no one to talk to, nowhere to turn to except the Lord—*so she did!* She prayed with all the doors of her soul opened wide to the risk of loving others through Christ.

She appropriated the power of the Holy Spirit and used the Resource Account to its fullest extent!

You can too! We all can!

LOOKING BACK

Over and over again the story my mother told about God telling another person to do such and such ... and that same child of God saying "No" ... has come back to teach and convict my mind and soul.

I wonder how many times the Holy Spirit has put a name and a thought about that person in my mind and I've reasoned:

1. I don't have time/money, etc. to get involved.
2. Their situation isn't desperate. I'll just say a quick prayer.
3. They don't need any help from me.
4. I'll give them my solutions. Not my time, money or comfort. Just some off-the-top-of-my-head solutions.

HEART OF THE MATTER

The Holy Spirit rarely talks to my heart in anything above a gentle whisper. I must tune in to that kind of listening so I won't miss the pure joyous pleasures of God working through me (imagine that!) or fail to lead another soul away from the dark path of doubting that God answers prayer.

SIX

The Refinement Account

Rick and Laurie's dog Popotla (we called him Popo for convenience) had a problem. Actually he had several problems, but the one I'd like to tell you about is a problem named August the Ninth. August was just a six-week-old kitten when Laurie compassionately brought him home to live with us. She and our church youth choir were performing at another church, and after the concert was over a *very smart* mother had her children standing by the church bus, holding six adorable little kittens. The children rolled their eyes in such a sad way Laurie scooped up the yellow one and got on the bus. (Five other kittens rode the same bus home that day.) But back to our dog.

Popo took one look at that little butterball of yellow fur, and, even though he towered above the kitten, Popo was *terrified*. The kitten, however, was actually delighted to see Popo. Just another *larger-type cat*, he thought. The kitten, August the Ninth, immediately wanted to show his friendliness and would have been delighted to have romped all day, except that Popo went into the first stages of a nervous breakdown. The dog withdrew to the corner of our family room and cried a lot.

In the weeks to follow I stopped a lot of activities to watch as that tiny ball of yellow fur name August reduced a good-sized dog into a whimpering, simpering, neurotic mess.

August chased him. Popo ran. August touched him. Popo shook. August pounced and attacked him. Popo jumped. August clung to his throat. Popo walked around, his eyes bulging out of his head and this "thing" swinging gently under his chin.

In short, Popo had *quite* a problem, and as I saw it, he had three options:

1. He could get mad. He could get absolutely vicious and kill that cat. I called the veterinarian who knows Popo and asked how much stronger the dog was than the kitten. "Immensely," the doctor said. "Popo could lift one paw and by setting it squarely on August the kitten, he could snuff him out like a small candle."

Had Popo been able to talk, he might have said to us, "How *dare* you do this to me?" Or, "How could you, a loving family, say you love me and at the same time let this yellow thing hassle me every minute of the day?" He really had a genuine right never to trust us again. Yet somehow he did not choose to get mad or lose his faith.

2. His second option was to ignore the cat completely. He could have gritted his teeth, admirably controlled his panic, and walked around like there was *no* August the Ninth. We would have admired that noble attitude even if ignoring a problem isn't too realistic. But Popo chose a third option.

3. He admitted he *did* have a problem. He decided that since August seemed destined to stay forever, he'd be thankful for him and *accept* him. For the first time since the kitten had started chasing him, Popo stopped, turned slowly around and faced the enemy straight on. August had never seen this tactic before and wasn't too well prepared for Popo's paw that swiftly but playfully knocked all four feet out from under him. After that it was fun and games for both of them. Once in a while the kitten got the best or worst end, but it usually worked out pretty even. Then, after some months, they were able to sleep side by side in relative peace.

I don't know what convinced Popo to tackle his problem head on, but he seemed to have things under control after he restructured his *attitude*. After acknowledging his problem, he began to *accept* his decision. I know animals are not supposed to be thinkers or have attitudes, but I think there was something vaguely and strangely human about Popo's and August's situation.

Many of us, when faced with problems, refuse in one way or another to *accept* them and instead take the first option— *anger*. Not too long ago I received a traffic ticket for following too closely. The policeman, as he handed me my copy of the citation, thanked me for being cooperative. He mistook my silence for cooperation. Actually, I was furious with the whole situation and didn't dare open my mouth for fear I'd spend the night in jail. It was the last straw in a very bad day! I was tired from singing in a recording session, it was late at night, and I had been trying to pass a lady in a winding canyon because *her* driving was so erratic. *She* should have gotten the ticket! I was angry with everything that night and particularly at the personal injustice dealt to me. Even though I didn't lose my temper, I certainly could not come up with one reason as to why the whole thing had happened.

David Augsburger, in his fabulous book on forgiveness,[1] talks about Jesus' anger and he says, "His anger was over principles of right and wrong, not over persons and personalities. Christ's anger was never motivated by personal abuse."

My anger that night was most certainly motivated by what I felt was personal abuse! I was angry at God, too, because all day I'd been about His work, and I was tired and spent when this happened.

We often wonder, *Why did this happen to me? Why is God doing this to me?*

Is it wrong to become angry about our problems? No. That's probably a fact of life. But it is wrong to take out our anger on others. The Scripture says, "Be angry, and sin not."

The night I got the ticket I should have said, "Okay, Lord,

what are You going to teach me from this one?" Later I'll share what happened the day I showed up in court to pay my fine.

The second option is to ignore the whole situation as if that will make it go away.

As long as we are alive and breathing, we will have problems that make us angry. Only the dead are finished with the daily problems of life.

My pastor, Ted Cole, preached frequently about our temporary heartaches, sufferings, and disappointments and he always referred to them as "heaven-sent refinements."

God uses the pain, the failures and the hurts of our lives and yes, even the anger as tools to help us grow spiritually. But we often prefer to shut our eyes and walk in denial of painful situations or destructive relationships.

Our third option is to accept and use our problems. That's God's solution, but it's a tough assignment.

I find myself falling right in line with tens of thousands of people who, when a problem presents itself, want *out, out, out!* I don't like rain on my parades, lumps in my gravy, or dirty diapers on my babies. The first thing I come up with is, "How soon can I leave and get away from all this?"

What astounds me about my attitude toward problems is that it is *completely opposed* to what is presented in the Bible.

When James says to me in his first chapter, "... is your life full of difficulties and temptations? Then be happy." (v. 2, *Living Bible*). I think, *Oh, come on, Brother James, are you kidding? Be happy when my washer breaks down? Especially since the washer always feels the need of a comrade, so the stove or water heater joins the strike against me at exactly the same moment? Be happy when my worst nightmare comes true? Be happy?*

Then James rubs salt in the wound when he says, "... and don't try to squirm out of your problems" (v. 4, *Living Bible*). Actually, I find I'm very happy about problems when I am squirming *out* of them, and running like a gazelle escaping from a fierce tiger.

James is truly convinced that these troubles will make us grow. I'm not sure I want to—not quite that much anyway—because growing always hurts.

How can I accept problems (from the tiniest to the largest) in life and how can I be happy during the refining process? How does anyone do that?

I think *acceptance* begins with taking a deep breath and one step back during the first moments of devastating news, of a relational conflict, or even of minor snafus. It is in that second that we, as Christians, can repeat with the Psalmist,

"Lord, you know the hopes of humble people. Surely You will hear their cries and comfort their hearts by helping them" (Ps. 10:17, *Living Bible*).

When I remember this verse I can *begin* (as difficult as it may be) to be "happy" as James describes. Of course, what makes living through the Refinement Account so difficult is that sometimes the pain is so sudden or so acute that most of us can't seem to wait to be "happy." Once again, I need to review the Psalms and take heart from words like these, "Don't be impatient. Wait for the Lord, and He will come out and save you! Be brave, stouthearted and courageous. Yes, wait and He will help you" (Ps. 27:14, *Living Bible*).

I have found that if I read the following verses to a group of Christian women, they'll be in wholehearted agreement. We believe, "No matter what happens, always be joyful, for this is God's will for you who belong to Christ Jesus" (1 Thess. 5:18, *Living Bible*). We also believe, "And we know that all that happens to us is working for our good if we love God and are fitting into his plans" (Rom. 8:28, *Living Bible*).

We can agree that we should *always* be joyful, we should *always* pray, and we should *always* thank God. We can agree that God controls even the minutest detail of our lives and that it all works together! All of us, to a woman, agree that these words are true ... *except* when we are in trouble. When we hear the doctor say, "cancer," when our child dies, when our best friend, pastor or counselor breaks our confidence, when our husband loses his job, then we Christian women fall apart just like our non-Christian neighbors.

I can be hard on these hypothetical Christian women because I've been caught in precisely the same trap many times. I thoroughly believe I'm to be joyful and really thank God for everything *until* something goes wrong. Then I do not "in everything give thanks," but rather I say like you, "Oh, why Lord? Why me?" It's a natural reflex and a human trait, for no one in their right minds look forward to experiencing the Refinement Account? Rather we pray ... "Lord, if this cup can be removed—remove it!"

I've been going to prayer meetings for years, yet I've never heard a Christian man or woman stand up and say:

"I thank the Lord because my daughter did *not* win the essay contest or get on the cheerleaders squad."

"I thank the Lord because my husband was just fired."

"I thank the Lord because our TV set broke, the washer broke, and we just found out our son has to have expensive braces on his teeth."

"I thank the Lord because my doctor told me today I have breast cancer."

"I thank the Lord because my child was murdered."

"I thank the Lord because my Christian boss has just cheated me out of two months' salary."

"I thank the Lord because my husband just asked me for a divorce."

"I thank the Lord because my husband has abused me or my children."

"I thank the Lord because I just found out my son is gay."

No, I've never heard these kinds of statements, even in small intimate prayer groups—and certainly *I've* never thanked the Lord for pain and suffering. Even the night I got the traffic ticket I never thought of thanking *anyone*, much less the Lord.

I could go on, but I'm sure you get the point and you can see the list is endless. Never, in all my years of being in or out of church, have I heard these kinds of "thank you's," yet God tells us in *everything* to give thanks.

David, the psalmist, was really convinced that problems and thankfulness were companions. He knew if he accepted the pain and suffering of the refinement process in his life and took on thankfulness as an attitude, he'd be able to bear the hurt.

David, in a song, wrote, "It is good to say, 'Thank You' to the Lord, to sing praises to the God who is above all gods. Every morning tell him, 'Thank you for your kindness,' and every evening rejoice in all his faithfulness" (Ps. 92:1,2, *Living Bible*).

Later, when things evidently were looking worse, he wrote, "I will praise the Lord *no matter what happens*" (Ps. 34:1, *Living Bible*).

Why don't we hear thanks to the Lord *no matter what happens*? Is it because bad things never happen to God's people? Of course not! We are all too familiar with the phrase "This is not fair!" We know too well that trouble, sickness, and disappointment fall on Christians and non-Christians alike. No one is immune to the unfairness and pain of life. Maybe the reason we don't hear too much about thanking God in adversity is that few of us *really* believe those Bible verses except when everything is going just fine ... or we are deeply into denial about pain and problems.

So perhaps hundreds of thousands of us go from one defeat to another because we find praising and thanking God is impossible to do when things go wrong or when life is so unfair.

I've read many books on thanking the Lord and they have touched me deeply. For a time. Why is it that for a while at least I'm stirred to thank God and then I forget? I wonder, will I ever come to the point of total commitment where, no matter *what* happens, I'll be so sure God is controlling each factor of my life and circumstances that I'll spontaneously thank Him for everything?

It was while we were vacationing in Baja, California one summer that I began, in a small way, to understand part of the reasons as to why I don't thank God for the bad as well as the good in my life.

Pastor Don Brandt and his family and our family shared the

joys of a little "casa" on the Pacific Ocean. Its remote Mexican charm was delightful and it always gentled our spirits. However, it did have *very* faulty plumbing.

That summer when I heard my husband yell, "Oh, for Pete's sake, not again!" I was pretty sure the toilet had come apart at the seams for the third time *that day*. Now here was a simple but real down-to-earth problem.

It wasn't directly *my* problem, so I could be quite objective and even a little smug as I called out, "Hey, in view of what I I've been learning about thanking God for my problems, do you think you could say, 'Thank you, Lord, the toilet has broken again'?" His reply was terse.

"No, Joyce, I don't think I'm spiritually up to it at this point!"

I thought about his answer and wondered, isn't that where we all live? Our spiritual batteries are charged up by a sermon, a book, or some music which stirs our hearts, and we burn brightly with enthusiastic gratitude. But as time passes we dwindle down from brightness to twilight and "spiritually we're not up to it" when problems or pain arrive.

It's so easy to thank the Lord for all the good and beautiful things. Just that week I had said aloud and prayed, in all sincerity, "Thank You, Lord, for the safe, fun trip down to our little Mexican house by the sea."

"Thank you, Lord, for the beautiful, sparkling, azure blue ocean and the marvelous brown pelicans that put on soaring flight demonstrations each day for us."

"Thank You, Lord, for the delicious handmade tortillas I buy at the little shop in Rosarito Beach."

But in all the years we went down to the casa, I never prayed or heard anyone in my family say, "Thank You, Lord. Isn't this great! We just ran out of butane gas for the stove and fridge." Or, "Thank You, Lord, for all that gooey tar that washed up on the beach which is clinging to everyone's feet and tracking all over the casa floors."

And certainly I've never heard anyone say, "Thank You,

Lord, I'm so glad it's *my* turn to do the dishes!"

The morning after the plumbing was all fixed (again) we had finished devotions and began talking about thanking God. My husband voiced his feelings by saying he really didn't know what good would have been accomplished if I had been able to thank God for the broken toilet.

I suddenly realized that because I had thanked God ... two things happened. Aloud I said, "But I did thank the Lord and when the plumbing was restored I was very glad the stupid thing conked out because it made me appreciate the *working* plumbing we have at home. Secondly, the thought that you were able to fix it without a plumber was a real source of satisfaction." We both smiled. It was no big deal, no big spiritual revelation. Or was it? Some of the most difficult things to thank the Lord for are the unexpected, the incidental and somewhat annoying problems or events. But even worse are the unfair or unjust things that come with being alive.

I became aware of an unjust situation which involved a dearly loved friend of mine. A nineteen-year-old college girl named Sue.

In early spring of one year she phoned me. Before she had finished saying hello it was obvious that she had been utterly devastated.

I asked her what in the world was wrong, and pouring out of her came the details of a conversation she had just had with her father. Sue's mother died a few years ago and her father had remarried. For some unexplainable reason he had phoned her and said quite casually that she was now on her own. His words had hit her like a ton of bricks. Her dad went on to say that even though she was his daughter she was no longer his responsibility. Sue was told to make her own decisions from then on. He also told her that since he had no place for her during the coming summer months in his home, she was to make her own arrangements for where she would stay until the fall semester.

She was sobbing and mumbling incoherently about how unfair it all was when she heard her father tell her that after all, *he* had been on his own, working and shifting for himself, when he was nineteen and he said she should do the same thing, implying that being totally on one's own was simply a normal thing. Long after he hung up she remained at the phone, utterly crushed and completely broken-hearted.

At first I was furious with her father. I knew this girl to be one of the most talented, lovable, conscientious students alive. She was truly given to being God's person. How could her dad say such thoughtless, cruel things?

I immediately remembered a scene from my past.

Once, long after I had grown up, I was visiting my mother and was pouring out some minor problems when suddenly I stopped and said, "Oh mother, I'm sorry to be burdening you with these problems. I'm a big girl and on my own now. I shouldn't be bothering you."

She reacted immediately and said in her sternest voice, "My dear girl, I don't care how old you get or how many years you are married, you will always be my girl, and you will never have to be on your own!"

The memories of that moment warmed me, but I couldn't bring myself to share it with this broken-hearted girl. The contrast was too great. Then I thought of my father-in-law. Even though he was in his seventies and my husband had been on his own for years, I knew that if we ever knocked on Dad's door and said, "We have nothing ... We've lost everything ... Can we come in and live with you?" the door would have been flung open with no questions asked, and we would have understood clearly we were not "on our own"! I couldn't share this with Sue either.

"Oh, God," I silently prayed, "here I am so furious with her father I can't be any help at all with this ugly angry spirit in me. Help me to give thanks for this inconsiderate man. Please give me the right words to bind and heal Sue's crushed heart." I found myself thinking about the verse "honor thy father and thy mother," so aloud, I reminded Sue that the commandment does not say we are to honor them because they are smart, or right, or beautiful, or anything else, but because they simply are our father and mother.

I recalled vividly an illustration Ken Poure had given to a group of high school kids at Hume Lake on this very verse. He told about a meeting in which he spoke on the subject of honoring your parents. Afterwards a girl came up to Ken and said, "I can't honor my parents ... and I never will." When he asked why, she told him this story.

Her parents had divorced and the courts awarded her and her three brothers to the mother for six months of the year and then to the father for the next six months. So they spent the first six months with their mother and then eagerly traveled, with the teenaged sister driving across the country, to begin the next six months with their father. They drove to the city, found the house, and were delighted to see their father standing on the porch across the street. The boys were so anxious to see their father that without thinking or looking up the street they jumped out of the car, ran across the street, were hit by a car, and were all killed. The young girl went on to say to Ken, "I'll get over their deaths in time ... What really gets me is this: I can never honor my mother and father because neither of them attended my brothers' funeral." Then God, as He often does, gave Ken the wisdom to tell this girl that perhaps she was the strong person she was because of this very thing. That perhaps God had allowed these horrible, unfair, and unjust things to happen to make her into His chosen vessel. That maybe, just maybe this was her time of refinement. Nothing had changed. The boys were dead and the parents hadn't attended the funeral. But the girl was being refined in a way that could forever change her life attitudes, views and potentials.

I related this story to my distraught Sue on the phone. I said, "Honey, if you can allow yourself to learn from this experience, to even *thank God* for this father who has treated you so unjustly ... who knows what can be accomplished by it? How do you know but that this is the very making of you?"

Since Sue was of such beautiful and sterling character, she quickly moved from panic to relative calm, looked realistically at the facts, and, although she understood none of her dad's words, actions, or intent, at that very moment she began to thank God. Acceptance began to form in her heart and mind.

Now I wish that I could write that two weeks later God honored Sue's faith and her father apologized deeply for his words, took her into his arms, and asked her forgiveness. But as a matter of fact, things didn't get any better, they got much worse.

Near the end of that semester Sue's stepmother called asking her what she would be doing during the summer. Sue explained that she could qualify at an out of state university for courses during the summer or stay at the college and try to get a job. Her stepmother responded, "Well, it's good you have plans, because you certainly can't stay with us. We don't have any room for you."

Hot tears filled Sue's eyes and her emotions shouted to her, "They don't want me ... they don't have any room for me ... I'm alone and nobody wants me."

A few hours later Sue came to my home. She had committed herself to thanking God for this whole painful mess. She stayed overnight on my living room couch, and once more the Lord brought joy in the morning. In fact, for the next few days He sent the balm of Gilead to soothe her troubled, wounded heart. His presence seemed to make up for the lack of parents and parental love. He surrounded her. The growing made her glow with beauty! Her time of refinement was showing.

The next few weeks were really wonderful. God gave Sue not one, but two sets of loving foster parents. They spent the summer lavishing on her all the love and prayers they could shower on her. She did more exciting, marvelous things in this summer of her life than ever before. She even managed to take several university courses and collected some needed credits. God healed her large wounds and even her small cuts. It had begun with thanking Him for such an unjust thing. But this is only a small part of what God accomplished that summer.

One day while Sue was attending summer classes, she did

something she'd never done before; she cut a class. Then, for some reason, she felt she should stay in her dorm room. About that moment a kitten ran past Sue's open door, made a circle, and ran scampering out. Sue chased it down the hall, and, before she knew it, the kitten had bounced through an open door, and she found herself in another student's room. The older woman was working on some papers, but she looked up, and recognized Sue. "Oh, Honey," she said, "I've seen you before and I've been wanting to get better acquainted with you! Sit down."

The conversation was easy, the woman gracious. Then, as in so many other Spirit-led discussions, the woman asked Sue to tell her about her background. So Sue sat there and innocently shared her life and her mother's death. Then, and only God knows why (because she was a quiet, almost shy girl), Sue shared her father's rejection and the telephone conversation she'd had with me about thanking God for everything. By the time Sue had neared the finish, the woman started to cry and little by little her tears changed to sobbing.

"How old are you?" the woman asked between sobs.

"I'm nineteen," Sue answered.

Then taking Sue's hand, the woman student told Sue about her background. In her case, her father had died, and it was her mother who had rejected her. The woman told of her inability to accept or honor her mother. Tearfully she confessed that she was fifty years old, the wife of a minister, and had never been able to face the ugly facts and forgive her mother. Nor had she ever thanked God. She was filled with wonder that Sue, at nineteen, could have learned such a lesson. Much healing went on between them that day there in the woman's dorm room. The conversation between these two was the turning point for the older woman. The decision to thank God in everything is costly, but it brings priceless dividends.

There is not a shadow of doubt in my mind that Sue's rejection by her father was the making of the girl. God used her biggest heartache to the maximum amount of good some six months later. I believe it was all locked up the moment Sue, so many months back, began to praise and thank God for her father's decision and response to her.

"Happy are those who have suffered persecution for the cause of goodness, for the kingdom of Heaven is theirs" (Matt. 5:10, Phillips' translation). Colleen Evans said of that verse, "Happy is the woman who can be unjustly criticized without jumping to her own defense." Happy, too, is the woman who can endure the most unfair event of all and not only accept it, but say, "Thank You, God, for this awful thing!" This woman is really rich! If the kingdom of heaven is this woman's, think of the real estate value tied up in her.

I know, firsthand, of one young college girl and one fifty-year-old woman who, because of thanking God for an extremely unjust thing, are immensely wealthy!

We all have the option of getting angry with God and shouting, "Why are You doing this to me?" But how much richer we can be if we learn to say, "Lord, what do You want me to learn from this?"

We can ignore our problems and deny that they exist. But acknowledging reality and its pain as part of life ... and then, *before* the smoke has cleared away, thanking God for it ... now, that's an experience!

Can you write down the hurt that is producing the most pain in your life right now? After examining it, try to see if there's a need to be forgiven or to *give* forgiveness. Then can you write, "Thank You, Lord, for this problem?" If you can, one of the first things that will happen is that the tense, tied-up feelings you have will give way to a strange unexplainable peace. Why shouldn't it? Doesn't God know all about the broken washer or the cancer surgery? If He knows about it, then He knows the ending too. Hasn't he promised us a peace that the world around us can't understand? Can you trust Him with that hurt today?

I can, and pain is a little easier to bear today when I've begun to deliberately thank Him. The bitterness seems to lift and my mind clears so much that the problem, while it might not go away, is more easily put into the right perspective.

A military wife in Hawaii was complaining to me about her terrible living quarters. She described the kind of housing she had left at the last post and how let down she was about this new location. In particular, the kitchen was a disaster area. I looked at her over lunch and said, "Dot, do you think you could thank God for that crummy kitchen?"

Well, she wasn't too eager and showed little confidence that she'd be able to do such a strange thing. But weeks after I returned from my speaking engagement at her military post I received this note from her. It said, "My kitchen is not *nearly* as crummy as I thought it was. Thanks to your visit to Hawaii." I could almost see her shoulders relax.

I wish I'd been closer to the Lord the night I got that traffic ticket. Physically it wouldn't have worked such a hardship on my nervous system, and mentally it wouldn't have scrambled my thoughts so badly. Had I been able to thank God, the whole situation might have been a bit more exciting. However, God had quite a plan in mind that night.

Three weeks later I went to court. I had to pay my almost-thirty-dollar fine in person, so I decided to talk with the judge. By then, I was thanking the Lord even though I really didn't think the whole thing was very fair. I'll never forget my experience in court.

After I told my sad story to the judge (he cut my fine in half), I realized with a jolt of recognition that this was the same judge and even the same courtroom where the trial was held for the men who had kidnapped and robbed my husband some three years before.[2]

I told the judge about my book, *His Stubborn Love,* and the story involving the kidnapping and asked if I could give him a copy. He said he'd love one, and we had a wonderful talk together with his assuring me he would read the *whole* book.

I went out to the car and brought back a copy of *His Stubborn*

Love. By that time the courtroom was crowded with people, so I simply walked over to the clerk's counter. Before I could say anything, six women clerks charged up to me and said, "Is that the book? What's it about?"

"Well, it's about a marriage that was finished and a God who gave a new marriage back to the same old people," I answered.

These six women and one judge all read about the witness of God's love. I could never have waltzed in there and said, "Hey, you needy people with such big problems ... let me tell you what God can do! And have I got a book for you!" Instead, God let me get a traffic ticket. And typically, I didn't thank Him or accept it until much later.

I believe God wants to do many marvelous things with the problems, disappointments, and losses He allows us to have; and we can trust Him, for He alone knows *which* problems and how many we can endure.

The Refinement Account is one we most naturally try to avoid—yet, once we experience the benefits, we find it's worth it. I think it's an account too precious to ignore.

Peter wrote, "After you have suffered a little while, our God, who is full of kindness through Christ, will give you his eternal glory. He personally will come and pick you up, and set you firmly in place, and make you stronger than ever" (1 Peter 5:10, *Living Bible*).

We can all draw from this account. We can even accept it and be grateful for it because *our God* has noted each deposit and withdrawal during our troubled, painful times. Peter's words are true. God will come, pick us up, set us firmly in place, and make us strong. Stronger than ever? Yes, that's the result of refinement.

David also knew a great deal about this account. He wrote:

Let all who are discouraged take heart. Let us praise the Lord together, and exalt his name.

For I cried to him and he answered me! He freed me from all my fears. Others too were radiant at what he did for them. Theirs was no downcast look of rejection! This poor man cried to the Lord—and the Lord heard him and saved him out of his troubles. For the

Angel of the Lord guards and rescues all who reverence him.

Oh, put God to the test and see how kind he is! See for yourself the way his mercies shower down on all who trust in him. If you belong to the Lord, reverence him; for everyone who does this has everything he needs (Ps. 34:2-9, *Living Bible*).

I think it's so like God not immediately to take David's troubles from him but, instead, to first free him from his fears. And best of all, if we draw from the refinement account, we'll know firsthand about angels guarding and rescuing us, about the mercies of God showering down on us, and about having our inner and outer needs met.

What an account! It's really a blank check, just waiting for our endorsement.

LOOKING BACK

When I contemplate the Biblical precept of "thanking God for *everything*," I understand just how unnatural this concept is for all of us. Also, I remember a story Corrie Ten Boom told me years ago. You may have read it yourself in her book *The Hiding Place*.

During the height of Hitler's Nazi regime, Corrie and her sister Betsie were interred at the Ravensbruck concentration camp. The holocaust was exploding around the Ten Boom sisters and some thirty five thousand other prisoners. The stench of death was overpowering, the hopelessness of starvation glazed their faces and the ghastly inhumane existence they were forced to endure are still, to me, incomprehensible. Yet, Betsie *was always* praising God and thanking Him for *all* things! She did it no matter what happened and she did it in spite of each new horror that violated and plundered her frail body and soul.

Once when a huge infestation of fleas invaded and overtook barracks #28 where they slept at night, it was Betsie who instantly (and cheerfully) insisted that both she and Corrie thank God for the fleas.

Corrie felt Betsie's "thanking God for all things" had gone

a bit too far. To Corrie, praising and thanking God for millions of horrid fleas was way above the call of duty or devotion.

But Betsie persisted. And Corrie's love for her sister won out. With a kind of teeth gritting determination, Corrie finally joined Betsie in thanking God for (of all things!) the fleas. Fleas? Yes. Fleas.

Sometime later Corrie was surprised, but not Betsie, to find that the reason they were able to have a service of prayer and Bible study (which was strictly forbidden) for all the women in the evening was that all the supervisors and guards *knew* barracks #28 had an overwhelming problem with fleas. No guard would set foot into this barracks, so Corrie and Betsie were free to hold their nightly services for the women. Many women, there, amidst the fleas, found hope and comfort in Jesus in the only barracks at Ravensbruck without routine inspection by the guards!

HEART OF THE MATTER

What strikes me so clearly today is that thanking God for all things isn't easy, convenient or natural. It wasn't for Corrie and Betsie ... and it's not for you and me.But they did it anyway. They found, like we can today, that God knows *exactly* what He's doing. He really has "planned out our days."

We can trust God with our gratitude and praise. He will not abuse that trust. He will not forget us, or abandon us. And one day His whole plan for us will become exceedingly apparent. We will sit back, as Corrie and Betsie did, shake our heads in wonder and say, "So that's what the fleas were all about!"

Corrie and Betsie Ten Boom, both with the Lord now, are not the only immensely rich children of God ... we are too!

[1] *Seventy Times Seven* (Moody Press, 1970)
[2] See Prologue to *His Stubborn Love* (Zondervan Publishing House, 1971).

SEVEN

The Millionaires Account

This book wouldn't be complete if I wrote only about *my* wealth, and certainly I should not give you the impression that the title, *Richest Lady in Town*, refers only to me. Actually, it includes thousands of women who are trying to be all that God wants them to be and who are daily discovering the riches which can be found in this exhilarating, exhausting, thrilling, yet scary at times life.

I've probably left some valuable accounts out of this writing, but I must not leave out this chapter about my millionaire friends. I am blessed with many millionaire friends. There's Bettye, Clare, Charlotte, Virginia, Ruth, Beverly, Eleanor, Martene, Judy, and many more; but let me zero in on just a few.

You probably have some friends like them, and maybe after reading about mine you'll understand what it is *exactly* that makes that certain friend of yours so priceless!

These women all lead different lives and are of various ages and life styles. But they all share a rather priceless ingredient: the spirit of forgiveness and mercy.

It's not just that they have been forgiven, but all of them have *accepted* that lovely forgiveness. They have seen clearly the plain fact that God *did* forgive them as He said He would, even though He knew every ugly, disappointing quality about them. Having accepted this forgiveness, they are free to forgive and give mercy and grace to others no matter how wonderful or horrible they might be.

Forgiveness and mercy shines and glows like a soft halo of light around each of these wealthy women. They seem to have taken Paul's words seriously when he wrote, "Be gentle and ready to forgive; never hold grudges. Remember, the Lord forgave you, so you must forgive others" (Col. 3:13, *Living Bible*).

In *Seventy Times Seven* David Augsburger describes forgiveness as *rare*, hard, and costly. As you read about my millionaire friends, you will see just how rare, hard, and sometimes costly forgiveness is, and yet how marvelously rich these women are!

One of these friends is a fabulous woman, the wife of a minister. I met her many years ago when I was the speaker for her church's mother and daughter banquet. Naturally I was seated at the head table right next to Pursilla Brandt, the minister's wife, and I was quickly advised to call her Perky.

From almost the first minute I turned to meet her I loved her. I was pretty dazzled by Perky's welcoming smile and gorgeous brown eyes. I had been to many mother and daughter banquets that month, so I was exhausted. But she refreshed my spirit so much that I'm sure I floated home instead of driving.

Perky was the exact opposite of the minister's wife I'd been with the evening before. During that dinner, before I spoke, I'd spent a miserable time trying to coax some conversation out of a depressed and angry woman who left me with the impression that she hated her husband in general and her husband's ministry in particular. The encounter had saddened my heart considerably.

All through my childhood I had a chance to observe my mother as a minister's wife and many other wives of pastors as they came through my dad's church and our parsonage. Then, after I was grown and as God allowed me to speak and sing in thousands of churches in the years to follow, I met, talked with, and got to know a multitude of pastor's wives. Though many of them were well-adjusted and happy, it seemed to me there was a growing number who were depressed and on the edge of despair, and their spirits were tinged with the pallor of bitterness.

I know and well understand that some of the problems ministers' wives face stem from the upheaval and trauma of constantly moving from one church to another. Then there are the dreary parsonages which, if furnished, are filled with Sister Brown's less-than-choice castoffs and painted by Deacon Smith who never did know the difference baby blue instead of navy blue would make on a bedroom wall.

Other problems arise because a woman married to a man of God is often expected to be totally picture perfect. Someone, I hope I never find out who, started the false legend that ministers' wives, once married to "God's answer man," have all the solutions and scriptures to everyone's hurts, and, while having no earthly problems of their own, are mature enough to take all suggestions, hints, and constructive criticism. And oh yes, she has her children whipped into such great shape that their behavior borders on a reason for nominating her to sainthood.

In real life we hardly know what to do with the poor pastor's wife who has any doubts or fears or suffers occasionally from the very human ailments of discouragement or depression. And my, how we talk, especially if her children misbehave, particularly *during* church! For then she will be told how to correct, handle, and rise above everything by any number of us well-meaning but eager-to-set-her-straight folks.

Long after I was grown, my mother asked my forgiveness for "some things" she had done during my childhood.

"What things?" I could hardly believe my ears.

Mother smiled and then told me about the time a photographer with McCall's women's magazine saw my mother and me in a department store. I was three years old with blond curls, hazel brown eyes and looking like a friend of Shirley Temple. The man asked Mother if he could photograph me for their magazine cover. Mother was thrilled and instantly told him yes. They set up the appointment for the following Monday morning. However, on Sunday when Mother told the story at church, a woman felt "led of the Lord" to speak up. She pointed out all sorts of sins connected with such a cover picture. The woman was convinced, as many were in that day, that still cameras and movies were on the same sinful level and that since $25 (a fortune!) would be given to the preacher's wife, that was taking the devil's money. On and on it went. So with that kind of pressure and applied guilt, Mother canceled the session.

When I asked her what she would have done differently had she had a second chance to be a minister's wife, she simply responded, "With every decision I had to make as a wife and mother I'd prayerfully go to the Lord and His Word. Then if I were sure I was not breaking any of His laws, I'd do whatever *I*, not Mrs. So-and-so, felt best."

Many people put the pastor's wife and their children up on pillars with far too unrealistic and unobtainable standards. They asked and expect too much of them as human beings. However, sometimes the wife or child of a preacher (myself included) have brought a great deal on ourself.

My friend Perky was a rare exception. She seemed fairly free from the usual hangups and discouragements others experience in being a minister's wife. She was and is a pure, enthusiastic, brown-eyed joy!

One time when I was under the dryer at our local hairdresser's shop, Perky tapped the top of my hot metal dome of a dryer and asked, "Hey, what are you writing so intently?"

"Oh, it's our anniversary," I replied. Then I went on to tell her that we'd been married seventeen years and instead of buying a card, I'd chosen to write a letter giving one reason for being grateful for each of those years.

Perky's response was darling and obviously she was inspired by this bit of news, because without any feelings of plagiaristic guilt, she stole my idea and wrote her own list for her and Don's anniversary. She called it, "Sixteen Reasons

Why I'm Glad To Be Called Mrs. Brandt." Here are some of
those reasons I stole from her for this chapter.

"1. Because I like sharing the name of not merely a 'big' person,
    but a 'great' person!

"2. I like the intimacy of hanging my toothbrush next to
    yours—even though you won't go modern with the elec-
    tric one.

"3. And, frankly, I like the 'cut of your jib and the swing of your
    rudder' (especially in that gorgeous blue suit you so
    reluctantly bought!).

"4. Who else can find a man *really involved* with other people
    and their problems who maintains a ready supply of
    humor constantly bubbling beneath the surface—just ea-
    ger for an opportunity to spring forth!

"5. And who can find a man who is such a patient listener and wise
    counselor, yet loquacious enough to 'fill in' awkward silences!

"6. And when you face *my* shortcomings with humor and put
    them last on the list of 'important' things in life, as though
    they were all so minor, it does make it easier for me to
    accept *myself!*

"7. I admire your courage and willingness to tackle the un-
    known—all of life is an adventure with you!

"8. It's a rare man who continues to treat his wife like a queen
    long after courtship, but after sixteen years, the acid-test of
    marriage has not tarnished your exquisite manners.

"9. I'm glad you don't consider marriage a 50-50 partnership,
    even though we've agreed it's a 70-70 proposition. It
    seems like you're giving more than half *most* of the time!
    (I'm sure the children will always remember the times you
    do their dishes for them. When I walk in and exclaim what
    a good job they've done, you never tell me *you* did it.They
    look just as guilty as a gangster's auditor!)

"10. I adore being your wife because it doesn't seem to threaten
    your masculinity to show compassion, especially toward
    your family. (You know, those spontaneous 'love taps'

just make my day!)

"11. Yes, I can hold my head high when someone says, 'Are you *Mrs.* Donald Brandt?' because that name stands for truth, courage, and joy from one who has an adept way of spreading it!"

You see, what did I tell you? Perky is quite wealthy! Part of her riches come from the fact that she really believes her husband is not the *only* one "called of God." She has clearly heard in her own heart her husband's call to the ministry but she has also listened as God has softly called her to be the "preacher's wife." And with all her might and soul Perky has responded "Yes!"

I think that in their years of marriage Perky has been able to forgive her husband for accepting the call of God to the ministry. Does that sound strange to you? It shouldn't, for we find sometimes while we deal with the nitty-gritty of life we may have to forgive others for good things as well as the bad. For instance, one of the biggest things Perky has had to forgive and accept about Don being a pastor is that their home is located on one end of the church parking lot and, on any hour or day of the week, twenty-five to thirty people *will* drop in. And that right there, in my thinking, gives her twenty-five or thirty reasons to forgive Don for being a minister. Perky and Don are still my friends and still rich beyond belief!

Another millionaire friend of mine is my sister, Marilyn. She continues to add, year after year, to my vast supply of wealth.

She is very beautiful inside and out—so much so that when she was a student at Azusa Pacific University in California they elected her their homecoming queen. The first time a freshman was ever elected as queen at APU.

The day after the crowning ceremonies I sat with her at the homecoming football game. I remember how beautiful she looked and how proud I was of her. She is twenty years younger than I and only a year and a half older than my son, Rick, so I rarely ever thought of her as my sister. (It was always

"Marilyn, my other child" and it was that way especially after our mother died when Marilyn was only fourteen.)

My then twenty-six-year old brother, Cliff, was Marilyn's escort that gorgeous sunny day. I'm sure the homecoming queen's crown *never* looked as beautiful on anyone's head as it did resting above her long, softly curled dark hair. Later when we were alone together I asked, "Marilyn-Honey, last night before they announced your name as the winner at the ceremonies, did you have any idea, with all those other beautiful girls, that you'd be queen?"

I'll never forget how Marilyn turned to me and almost with a trace of guilt said quietly, "Oh, Joyce, you know what? I knew I'd be chosen a few minutes *before* they announced it."

I thought so! Marilyn hadn't looked a bit surprised when they made the announcement and placed the crown on her head.

"You really KNEW?" I questioned. "How did you know?"

Quietly she said, "Yes. I just *knew*." Then Marilyn related that three weeks before, during her devotions, the Lord asked her if she would give up something. Marilyn never did tell me *what* it was other than that it was something very special to her. She went on, "I told the Lord 'Yes, I'd give that up.' Then He showed me something else and asked the same question and I swallowed hard, but I said, 'Yes.' Then He asked me to give up a *third* thing, only this was something I *really* loved, so it took a little longer, but in the end I said, 'Yes, Lord, even that.'"

Then, Marilyn spoke thoughtfully as she said, "Then the Lord said, 'Marilyn, three times I've tested you by asking you to give up something and three times you've *willingly* said yes. Now, I'm going to give you three yes's back.'"

Marilyn continued by saying, "Joyce, two weeks later the representative from the freshman class formally asked me to be one of the twelve girls competing for homecoming queen. I heard the Lord's spirit in my heart saying at the end of that day, 'That was your first yes.'

"One week after that I was chosen to be one of the five

finalists. During my prayer time that night I heard the Lord confirm, 'That was your second yes.'

"Finally," Marilyn's eyes danced with joy, "Oh, Joyce, the night of the crowning none of us knew who would be queen. We were all waiting for the master of ceremonies to make the announcement. I was on the stage in line with the other girls when, in my heart, I heard the Lord clearly say, 'Marilyn, I'm about to give you your third yes.' I didn't have to wonder what ... I just knew what He was about to do."

Marilyn had claimed nothing nor begged for anything. She had even been willing to lose three very dear things, and because of her dear God-trusting heart the Lord bestowed a most delightful honor on her.

Marilyn is rich, you see, in accepting the attitude and stance of *trusting* and *obeying* God. It's really hard for some of us to remember that most of God's promises to us depend on those two words. But it's quite an exchange! Think of this, we trust Him and obey Him; He gives us riches and treasures *beyond* our hope. Marilyn gave Him those two words and He rewarded her with a remarkable inner wealth.

Once I asked her to tell me the exact circumstances in which she wholeheartedly gave her life to the Lord. We had been raised to love Jesus all our childhood, but I wondered when she had taken the deliberate steps to make the Lord her very own. She told me this event happened just hours after our mother's funeral. Marilyn had been fourteen, frightened, and unbelievably hurt and bewildered by mother's death. Over and over again she believed that Mother, even though she'd had a mastectomy three years earlier, would be healed of cancer. But that night, after Mother was laid to rest and friends and relatives had left, I had gone home with my own family. My brother, Cliff, had boarded a military jet and begun the journey back to Vietnam, and my father had stumbled wearily to bed.

Marilyn told me of going into the den and there, realizing her aloneness, she asked God to be her Friend, Savior, and

Comforter. In short, she decided to do an incredible thing. It boiled down to this. She *forgave* the Lord for taking her mother. He, in turn, began to melt the hurt and the bitterness. Marilyn's torn heart began to heal. In those moments following Mother's funeral and feeling very much alone, Marilyn started to become the beautiful and wealthy woman we so dearly love.

When I think of her, at such a young age, forgiving the Lord for mother's death, I remember the widow who said angrily to me, "Just how am I supposed to be thankful for my husband's death two years ago?"

I told her she'd *never* get over his death (or come to closure as they say now) until she could get to grief acceptance. She stood before me, some two years after her husband's death, still shaking her fist in God's face demanding to know why He had done this terrible thing to her. We will always be spiritually poor until the lesson of forgiveness melts our grieving hearts and begins its healing.

Marilyn is rich because her forgiveness is up-to-date and she's determined to be the woman God wants her to be.

Another millionaire friend is Sheila. Knowing her has been and still is an enriching experience. She continually adds to my wealth.

We attended the same church, First Baptist of Pomona, California. I was a wife and mother and had a daily radio program called, "Here's Joyce." One day as I was trying to get a mountain of household tasks done, my husband asked me if I needed someone to help with the housecleaning. I glanced over at my desk, took a long look at the stack of letters I was determined to answer, and suddenly put into words what had been rattling around my head as just a vague idea.

"You know, a housekeeper isn't what I need ... I desperately need a secretary." I almost surprised myself because I'd never really thought about having help at home or having help for my broadcast. I had no idea how much I would need a secretary, how I'd find one, or even how much it would cost. Yet there I stood, realizing that as I checked my mental priority list the top line shouted, "Secretary ... now!"

That night I earnestly prayed about a secretary. I said something like this, "Lord, You know I don't have the faintest idea if I even need a secretary really, except for someone to answer the mail. (I wasn't writing books yet—only doing a daily radio show.) Lord, I don't know how to find a secretary or how many days a month I'd need one ... but it seems clear that I should talk to You about it."

Then as I've prayed so many times down through the years, I asked the Lord to send a secretary to me ... especially since I didn't know where to begin.

The very next morning the phone rang. It was my friend Sheila, calling from our church office. She was checking with me about some church business. Being thoughtful, she stopped mid-sentence to say, "Oh, maybe you're busy ... should I call back later."

"Oh, no," I assured her. And I went right on to say, "I'm just sitting here at my desk trying to answer fifty letters from my radio listeners." By that time my daily syndicated radio show was producing an ever increasing volume of mail and it was beginning to be somewhat overwhelming. I went on about the load of correspondence for a while longer when Sheila said, rather quietly, "Why don't you let me help you with it?" I barely heard her and offered, "Oh, no ... I don't want to bother anybodywith ... " I stopped mid-sentence. *What am I saying?* I thought. Here I had prayed just last night for the Lord to please send me a secretary. Now I was on the phone saying, "oh, no," to Sheila who had been an executive's secretary for four years!

As the fog in my head cleared up a little I heard Sheila's voice sweetly saying, "Joyce, I've been praying ever since Darin was born that the Lord would let me use my typing and shorthand on a part-time basis so I wouldn't lose my touch or my secretarial skills."

Feeling somewhat silly, I pulled myself together and asked, "Would you be my secretary?"

"Yes, I'd love to," came Sheila's instant answer.

There are many factors in God's plans for our "abundant" lives, but I'm sure that one was Sheila's forgiveness being complete in the Lord. She was totally free to accept her life. She went from executive secretary to being a wife, mother, and homemaker. She did it with joy and there was nothing lost in the transition. Yet, the Lord had given her the intellectual wherewithal to develop her natural secretarial skills, and when the timing was right in my life He provided my need as the exact outlet she needed. Her secretarial skills were sharpened and more importantly kept alive. Sheila handled both her family and household chores along with her secretarial job for me and was completely comfortable and successful in both areas.

The only disagreement we've ever had in all the years we worked together was: did the Lord answer *my* prayer or Sheila's? (*I say mine!*)

One Thanksgiving she made me rich again by a short note. Sheila delivered it to my son, Rick, at our front door. She didn't come in, just handed it to him with, "Here, Rick, give this to your mother."

The note said:

"Happy Thanksgiving!

"I decided you're due for a note, so here's my Thanksgiving list for you:

"I'm thankful for you ...

"1. Because nearly every time we talk you leave me with some new, lovely, strengthening, or growth-producing thought to ponder.

"2. Because sometimes you sing a song for me—just me. I thought all day about the one, 'I was in His mind.' Then the Lord gave me the verse to go with it, Ephesians 1:4.

"3. Because I learn so much from the things I type.

"4. Because you must be the classiest person I know, yet the only one I know who wears bobby sox with her flats. You make me laugh ... [Come on, Sheila, it was cold that day!]

"5. Because I'm so proud to say, 'Thank you. Joyce *made* it or *gave* it to me.'

"6. Because you bring such pretty flowers to my house to brighten my day.

"7. Because it's fun to come to your house and enjoy your friends—that's why I'm so quiet. I'm enjoying everyone's conversation.

"8. Because I loved typing chapter one of *The Richest Lady in Town*. All right—you may well *be* the richest lady in town, but I'm wealthy too because I have the Lord *and* you!"

The next time you think you have to spend a fortune on a gift for a friend, remember Sheila's priceless letter to me and write your own to someone you love. It will be much more impressive than an expensive gift elegantly wrapped, and it will last forever!

I have been made wealthy by the strength of character, surrender, to the Lord and to the ministry I see in another friend. Her name is Ruth Calkin. She and her husband Rollie were and still are dear friends.

Ruth has writing talent—I mean real, gifted writing ability. A note, a card, one of her mini-moods (poems) or *anything* Ruth writes is a deep source of wealth to me.

As I have been in the public eye most of my life many people have sent or given me their writings, songs, poems, articles, and manuscripts. I've looked at all of them. Some are great, some are incredibly bad, some are just routine, even a little boring; but I've enjoyed even the bad ones because the people took time to write their thoughts down on paper. (Millions of sincere men and women say they are going to write a book, but very few really do.)

But Ruth's writing ... that's always different. Her way with words takes my breath away! Whether she writes a serious letter, a thank-you note, a prayer, a poem, a song, or whatever, it always touches me deeply ... so deeply in fact that it takes a while to recover.

A friend once said, "Ruth's thank-you notes are the only

ones in the world that require writing a thank-you back!"

Her letters written to hundreds of people during the past years have given great comfort and joy. Her Christmas gift to me one December was, like her, truly rare. No other gift gave me so much that year. It was a folder of Ruth's "mini-mood" thoughts. And just so you'll get a sampling of her wonderful ways with words, here is what she wrote on the front page,

"Dear, dear Joyce:

"One day at the beauty shop you asked if I had been writing. I told you no, because there was no other true answer. However, I have—from time to time—been jotting down 'mini-moods.' Little bits of prayer and reflection that have suddenly just 'been there.'

"You would laugh if you could see the scraps of paper and envelopes and registration cards and corners of grocery sacks I had to gather together in order to type these for you, but somehow I wanted so much to do it!

"Perhaps you'll remember that several years ago I gave you the story of Sam for your birthday—along with other story outlines. That memory keeps coming back to me this Christmas season. And again, I'm suddenly overwhelmed with a sort of ache to share something with you not found at a store counter—something that says, 'I am Ruth and I want very much to give part of me away to Joyce this Christmas.' The reason is simple: Just my gratitude and love.

"So here is my special, personal gift to you. Out of many moods I have chosen these few with tender loving care!

"May your Christmas be—

All Joy!
Ruth"

Of all the mini-moods in that folder, this one was my favorite because at that time I was on stage both in radio and for many singing and speaking engagements. Ruth entitled it *Who Will Clap For Me?*

I am often dramatic
Sometimes ecstatic
In the role I play
On the stage of Life
I bow
And smile
And bask
In the limelight,
Hoarding each moment
Of thunderous applause,
But when the curtain is pulled
For the last time,
When the crowds have dispersed
And the stage is dark,
Who will clap for me then, Lord?
You?

Ruth's writing, as always and particularly in these past years, has a rare freshness. And if this was all there was to her wealth, you might be asking, "So she's talented, that's nice. I'm glad for her, but so what?"

It's just this. Every time I read something of Ruth's I think, *Wow, I wish I'd written that,* or *I wish the Lord had said that through me.* In short, I wish I had her talent. However, I'm not sure that if I had her talent I'd still be hanging in there writing. For although God gave Ruth a truly gifted mind which is able to express itself through her writings, for a very long time few of them were published. And people may have never read any of her powerful and poignant words.

Had I been put through the same scenarios, I believe I would have quit writing long, long ago. I think I would have broken every pencil in half and confined my writing to postcards which said, "Having a wonderful time. Wish you were here."

Ruth had every right to do a number of things; get discouraged, then mad, quit or become bitter and blame God for not opening a publisher's door for her. Yet she remained obedient to what she knew God wanted her to do which was, *write*. Sure, she had a few things published over the years, but not nearly what could have been until after many, many years of pouring out her heart on paper.

Actually, to me, it seemed that whether or not Ruth would ultimately be published was not her largest concern or priority. She had been given a ministry which for many years meant just writing letters and notes to individuals. It was a unique journey and without visible fame or financial rewards, yet Ruth kept on writing.

I am one of the hundreds of people she writes to every year. Ruth's direct contact with the Lord and the gift of expressing on paper what is needed is phenomenal. It may be a quick poem in the center of the page or a long detailed letter, but her letters arrive at the right time and somehow she meets my precise need. Now— with her many books being published and distributed all over the world—all of us are enriched by Ruth as she continues to let the Holy Spirit lead her. You've probably seen her works at the bookstores, but even if you haven't, in heaven's library the card file clearly indicates that *Ruth is published*.

Another friend I'd like you to meet is an Army chaplain's wife named Carolyn. To me she is the epitome of the beatitude that says, "Happy are the utterly sincere, for they will see God" (Matt. 5:8, Phillips' translation).

Carolyn is completely honest with herself, her husband, family, friends, and above all, God. And what may be most important, she has forgiven the U. S. Government, the Pentagon, the Army, and the Military Chaplains' Corps. This must be true as I've never heard her complain about the negative vicissitudes of military life.

Colleen Evans wrote unknowingly of my friend, Carolyn, when she described the "utterly sincere" as "... the woman who gives every conscious area of her life to God, and goes on to ask Him to reveal areas of the subconscious that need to be healed and given over. There is no inner tension in this woman, for she seeks to hide nothing from God or man."

Carolyn lives her life as the wife of a military officer (now retired) in that kind of honesty, and consequently others are not aware of her inner tensions even if she does, in fact, have some. Actually, one of her loveliest traits is her well-developed, marvelous sense of humor. She is such a joyous comedienne she makes me smile, giggle, and down-right howl, yet I have also wept with her in prayerful moments. As I continue to say, having a sense of humor really boils down to this fact; we don't take ourselves *dead* seriously. What happens to you, big events or small annoyances, are probably not really of earth-shaking importance in the light of nuclear meltdown, homelessness and hunger gripping our world. But this kind of evaluating takes honesty.

Carolyn is also one of the few women I know who acts her age without sobbing about it. She doesn't try to act or dress like some young chick but has *gracefully accepted* her age. That may not sound like any big deal to you, but, from all the conversations I've heard at women's meetings, age is one thing *very* few women have on their "most wanted" list. I think our society reveres older men but tends to ridicule older women. Carolyn, with a married daughter and a younger son, adopted the attitude that she is exactly the age God wants her to be. She's not a moment older or a moment younger than she should be. Growing older should not be a threat to the Christian woman who securely understands she's loved by Christ.

When I spoke and sang on two military tours for the Chaplains' Division in the Far East, I needed the rich gifts that Carolyn so lovingly gave to me in Okinawa. One was the gift of laughter, and believe me, doing 35 performances to 8,000 people in 21 hectic days of touring, I needed a laugh. The other gift was Carolyn's honesty which freed her from negative attitudes and inner stress. She refreshed my weary spirit in a hundred ways with these two gifts, and, even though the years have piled up since Okinawa, Carolyn's gifts still creep into my memory at odd times, and I smile because I'm blessed and warmed all over again!

There are a number of women I've observed over the passing of time who are millionaire friends of mine. Space does not allow for all their stories. Some like Corrie Ten Boom, Henrietta Mears, and Mary Crowley are with the Lord now ... but my, how rich they were! Then there is Clare Bauer and Barbara Johnson, each of them my present day millionaire friend.

Here is one last entry about a millionaire friend. Her name is Mary Korstjens and she's *very* rich! And her ways have made me rich. For instance, when I went overseas to sing and speak for the Army chaplains one year, it was Mary who wrote a letter to my children. It was a beautiful letter in which she thanked them for letting me go so far away, and she closed her letter with many encouraging words to help keep them from getting too lonely.

Mary's understanding, warm letter was the *only* one my children received from anyone although there were literally hundreds of people who knew I'd be gone. Mary, and Mary alone, had the foresight and the insight to write. It was a most priceless gift to me, but it was even more precious to Rick and Laurie as they knew Mary was paralyzed by polio from the neck down, and her handwritten letters involved a super-human amount of effort!

When a young wife and mother, Mary, was stricken with both spinal and bulbar forms of poliomyelitis. That she sur-vived at all was only one of God's miracles. Many other women, men, and children died. That her young minister husband, Keith, stayed by her side through the long thirteen months she lived, (no, existed) in an iron lung was equally spectacular. There were sixteen women in Mary's ward who had been stricken with polio that year. Almost all of them watched in dismay as their marriages dissolved. Some hus-bands never again showed up in the hospital once they heard the doctor's diagnosis of polio.

Mary, Keith, and their two little children, Ken and Karen, began living life in a completely different manner. Slowly they began to understand that their lives would never be as they had been or had planned.

When Mary was finally able to emerge from the iron lung she was brought home. But she came home to pick up her life completely paralyzed. Now she was to take up life as a woman, a wife and mother without the ability to move, sit, walk or take care of herself.

It was soon after Mary came home from the hospital that the truth of how her life would then be really hit Keith. All illusions as to the way he would like things to be vanished. It happened when Karen, then two and a half years old, fell down while playing outside. Karen did what all children do. She ran to her mommy, sobbing and holding up her skinned knee to be kissed.

Keith's mind and eyes photographed the scene indelibly. In shocked silence he watched as Mary, for the first time, understood and realized that she could not pick Karen up. She could not bend over her, hug her, or kiss Karen's hurt away. She could not lift her little girl to comfort and console her as she had always done. In fact, Mary knew she'd never again be able to do the routine, normal, everyday things required of mothers with children. All those skinned knees, the huggings, the holdings, and the kissings now had to be left undone. Strange, but those are all privileges I've taken for granted most of my life as a mother. As Keith described these moments he said the scene shattered his heart. He wondered how they'd ever pull themselves together. But a most unlikely thing began to happen. Keith was soon to find that a new Mary was emerging. She was far more quiet now but was beginning to show some amazing new strengths. She was to become incredibly strong.

It must have been at this time, during the early days of the trauma of polio and the paralysis, that Mary did some exploratory surgery deep within her own soul. I don't imagine it was easy for her—nor do I see myself able to do what she did.

Faced with the same set of circumstances, I might not have been able to do what Mary did, but somehow she managed to lay her stiffened body in the arms of God, and in those moments the Mary her husband, children, family and friends might never have seen began to slowly take shape. I believe that had it not been for the crippling and paralyzing disease called polio, we might have missed this amazing woman.

I believe Mary's beautiful life came into its own like a butterfly coming out of its cocoon when she forgave God for polio. Her anger and bitterness were replaced by a quiet spirit and a peaceful joy, and springing out of Mary's inner soul came a well of wisdom so rare that all who knew her were stunned by it.

Both Keith and Mary have taken this tragedy and all that transpired, including the bitterly hard turn of events it produced, and for all these years together have turned it, daily, over to God. It has not been easy. It is often the opposite of fun, and their life will never again be what they dreamed about as young lovers. Yet, what they have is so much more! Their accumulated wealth is massive! Having lived through these years Mary and Keith have known, seen, and experienced dimensions of God that few of us in an entire lifetime will ever see.

Besides that, their trauma has uniquely equipped them with all the credentials they need to minister to others. I think it's interesting to note that when my heart is breaking, I call them. When I wish I had some directions about my children, I call them. When I'm faced with unbearable pain, I call them. When I need objective thinking, I call them. Why? Because they are the biggest bank of help I've ever known. They have enormous holdings in trust, great wealth in obedience, and in the face of insurmountable odds, they are rich in praise of our Lord.

Because their ability to forgive is so clearly established, they are freed to be the people God wants them to be. Mary's gentle faith continues to smother out the flames of her own and our self-centered resentments.

These Godly people have survived one crisis after another,

from Mary, just this past year, being temporarily returned to an iron lung to the constant, never ending search for *another* nurse/housekeeper combination.

But in the years I've known Mary, the closest I've heard her come to complaining was one day when, rather wistfully, she said, "Just sometimes, I wish I could pick up my toothbrush and brush my own teeth." (Another privilege I've taken for granted all my life!)

Mary and Keith know more about the words "flexibility" and "adjustment" than any people I've ever met. Polio has been a refining element in their lives and they have come forth as pure gold.

Once, during the days of my writing this book, Keith sat across from me in my living room, his face wet with tears, as he spoke tenderly and glowingly of his quiet Mary. "I've said it publicly," he was saying, "and it sounds so editorial. We ministers get like that sometimes ... yet it's true. Mary, very soon after polio struck, began to show and exhibit an amazing strength. This quiet, soft-spoken woman's character began to surface as a towering strength, and not only that, but she was given a most beautiful child-like faith that in these years has been utterly unshakable!"

Later I received a note from Keith. He wrote of Mary's faith, "She doesn't talk in golden glowing phrases about it ... that's not her gift. She just *lives* it! And how she enriches my life! The tenderness and gentleness that I believe God has brought to my ministry, He has given to me *through Mary!*"

The Korstjen's have lived with the deep sorrow and desperate disappointment of Mary's illness (although they never speak of it as such) with so much steady courage and deeply imbedded joy that whenever I read, "How happy are those who know what sorrow means, for they will be given courage and comfort!" (Matthew 5:4, Phillips' translation), I think of *them*.

Mary and Keith saw in their lifetime the death of their dreams, plans and a whole way of life they thought they'd have. Yet I know them to be content, even happy, in the secure knowledge that God continues to control every facet of their journey here on earth. It is He who has helped Mary master the art of staying alive. It is His power that has given her such strong willpower. The doctors are amazed that Mary's atrophied leg muscles can now take slow, small, but sure steps. It is *His* grace and courage that helps her to endure and adapt to the braces and captive metal fittings that give her some limited measure of control over paralyzed arms and legs. Mary never seems to loose sight of the hope God has put within her, and because of that captivating, shining hope within her, she is a very rich friend indeed!

When I think of Keith and Mary and see them in my mind's eye, I can also see the words found in Psalm 34:22 which declare, "The Lord redeemeth the soul of His servants: and none of them that trust Him shall be desolate."

And I know Keith and Mary are the Lord's servants ... and millionaires!

These millionaire friends seem to have one thing in common in their lives: forgiveness. A forgiveness that works in two distinctly different ways; they have accepted God's forgiveness and they are committed to forgiving others. That's probably how they opened their brim-full accounts in the Bank of Heaven.

Just think! If we know Christ, if He has forgiven us our sin and we have asked Him to live inside us, we too, have the Bank of Heaven as our main supply and source of wealth. In fact, we have at least one priceless gift, the one of eternal, everlasting life. If we stopped right there we'd be far richer than many people, but *we mustn't* stop there.

Yes, while it's true that Christ came to give us His eternal life, He also came to give us abundant life right here and now ... life that overflows with riches ... even if your name is Mary.

I spoke at one of the many (and it felt like thousands) mother and daughter banquets this year about the need for God's forgiveness in our lives and our need to forgive others. A number of months later, Ruth, the pastor's wife, told me she had left the banquet that evening just glowing because she was so certain her forgiveness was up to date and all taken care of. She drove her daughter home, changed clothes, and then went back to the church to help the women clean up. As she worked she was silently congratulating herself on being so spiritually right. But as Ruth was in the middle of verbally patting herself on the back, she suddenly heard the Lord whisper, "What about your mother-in-law?"

"Oh her," she responded and went on wiping off a table. "Well, I've forgiven her, Lord, you know that!"

"Then why do you bring her into conversations and talk about her the way you do?" the Lord quietly persisted.

She halted her table cleaning and realized that it was true. She recalled that anytime anyone related an awful-thing-my-mother-in-law-did story, she had managed to top it with a bigger and better one about her mother-in-law.

That night the Lord brought such conviction that Ruth asked God's and her mother-in-law's forgiveness. She has lived and coped with her mother-in-law ever since, but she has been given the freedom to really love her, best of all, to keep still when others talk about *their* mothers-in-law.

I know, you're right; that is a small issue compared with Mary's illness, but both women have learned about the benefits on both sides of forgiveness. We all can.

Right now, keep in mind that if we have asked God to forgive us, *He has.* He promised that He would not only forgive us but forget whatever we confessed; and God cannot lie. So if we've asked, He has heard and *done it!*

Now, we must accept it. We need to stop hemming and hawing around. It's free. Take it. Let's not remind God of how awful or undeserving we are or what disgusting sins we have committed. That just wastes time. God already knows all about us and He has forgiven, so let's accept it. Forgiveness is ours.

That will free us to *forgive* others, even our enemies. It will also free us to *accept* people as they are without trying to make them into what we wish they would become. But most of all it will allow us to truly reach out and *love not only the lovely but the unlovely as well.* I have found that even the incredibly bad circumstances and people who have inflicted pain on us can be loved under these conditions.

We can spend our lives paralyzed, not by polio, but by bitterness, anger, even apathy, or an unforgiving spirit. But that's such a waste. The Lord waits with vast bank accounts called forgiveness and healing and our names are on the signature cards.

So, with all this in mind, let's climb out of our ruts of hopelessness. We should get up from the chair marked "poor me." We should put away our picture albums and memories of past failures. We must not let the hideous infection of bitterness and anger keep our wounds from the healing they so deserve. We must accept and trust the Lord about the "whys?" of our painful circumstances and put down those large boxes of worry, fear, and high anxiety. We don't need to carry their heaviness around!

We have a great God! We were born to live life with all its vexing peculiarities and its stressful and painful twists and turns. God knows each of our tolerance quotas. He won't bend us past our breaking point. Furthermore, when we were born the second time, we were automatically born into His great kingdom. The King is our Father! Our rights, our inheritance and our access to Him are ours because *we belong to Him. We are His child, His heir!* Think of it ... my Father and yours is the King!

Paul's prayer in Colossians 2 is my prayer for you. Every time I read it, a loud, happy, clanging bell starts to ring inside me.

This is what I have asked of God for you: that you will be encouraged and knit together by strong ties of love, and that you will have the *rich* experience of knowing *Christ* with real certainty and clear understanding. *For God's secret plan, now at last made known, is Christ himself.*

In him lie hidden all the mighty, untapped *treasures* of wisdom and knowledge.

I am saying this because I am afraid that someone may fool you with smooth talk. For though I am far away from you my heart is with you, happy because you are getting along so well, happy because of your strong faith in Christ. And now just as you trusted Christ to save you, trust him, too, for each day's problems; live in vital union with him. Let your roots grow down into him and draw up nourishment from him. See that you go on growing in the Lord, and become strong and vigorous in the truth you were taught. Let your lives overflow with joy and thanksgiving for all he has gone.

Don't let others spoil your faith and joy with their philosophies, their wrong and shallow answers built on men's thoughts and ideas, instead of on what Christ has said. For in Christ there is all of God in a human body; *so you have everything when you have Christ*, and you are filled with God through your union with Christ. He is the highest Ruler, with authority over every other power (Col. 2:2-10, *Living Bible*).

Have these truths really broken through the din of terrible noises surrounding our lives right now? Can we grasp this wonderful truth ... and live it? I think we can! Remember, *"You have everything when you have Christ!"*

Just this morning, as I was absorbing Corinthians, one verse jumped out at me. It shouted,

"You know how full of love and kindness our Lord Jesus was: though he was so very rich, yet to help you he became so very poor, so that by being poor he could make you rich" (2 Cor. 8:9, *Living Bible*).

How rich He was! Yet He gave it up, and through His sacrifice, we were made rich!

LOOKING BACK

I only wish I had the page space to include more of the millionaires who have blessed not only my life, but many others as well.

In viewing these beautiful people I believe there's a common thread running through all their lives. It seems to me they understand the concept of sowing and reaping extremely well!

We all get what we give. It's true. We really do reap what we sow, and in my mind's eye the millionaires I see are undoubtedly the most generous "sowers" I've ever known!

The Apostle Paul said it so well, "He who sows sparingly will also reap sparingly, but he who sows bountifully will also reap bountifully" (2 Corin. 9:6).

Ruth Calkin, one of my longtime favorite millionaire friends, put this concept best when she wrote ...

THE GREAT INVESTMENT

I praise You, dear Lord
For teaching my husband and me
To make friends with the money
You have entrusted to us.
We have so little to invest
In stocks and bonds
But so much to invest
In lonely, empty lives.
And, Lord, the rate of interest
Is enormously high.
In fact, as we continue to invest
The interest goes up and up and up![1]

HEART OF THE MATTER

It's time we woke up each morning realizing it. It's time we knew it and acted on it, especially if things are scaring us and going all wrong for us. It's true. We do have *everything* when we have Him!

At the risk of sounding like a woman who should be off to what Barbara Johnson calls the "Home for the Bewildered", I think it's really about time we threw open the shutters of our hearts, pulled out all the stops on our vocal chords, and yelled over to the neighbors next door, the people uptown and downtown, and to the whole world in general—"Hey, look at *me*. I have everything, and praise God, you know what? I'm the richest lady in town!

"That's right, *me*!

"*I'm* the richest lady in town!"

[1] From: *Lord, Don't You Love Me Anymore*, p. 119
  By: Ruth Harms Calkin © 1988
  Used by permission of Tyndale House Publishers, Inc.
  All rights reserved.

ABOUT THE AUTHOR

Joyce Landorf Heatherley is known nationwide as a uniquely gifted Christian communicator, able to convey Biblical principles with relevance, humor, compassion and gentle conviction--in a way that speaks to the needs of men and women from all backgrounds. A best-selling author of both fiction and non-fiction, her 23 books include: MY BLUE BLANKET, THE INHERIT-ANCE, BALCONY PEOPLE, SILENT SEPTEMBER, MONDAY THROUGH SATURDAY, FRAGILE TIMES, IRREGULAR PEOPLE, HE BEGAN WITH EVE, CHANGEPOINTS, UNWORLD PEOPLE, MOURNING SONG, JOSEPH, I CAME TO LOVE YOU LATE, FRAGRANCE OF BEAUTY, and RICH-EST LADY IN TOWN.

Joyce is also an immensely popular speaker and conference leader. Recordings of her more popular talks, including: BAL-CONY PEOPLE, IRREGULAR PEOPLE, UNWORLD PEOPLE and THE INHERITANCE are available on audio cassette, as are video tapes of CHANGEPOINTS, IRREGULAR PEOPLE, and UNWORLD PEOPLE. Her HIS STUBBORN LOVE film series, based on her nationally acclaimed seminars of the same name, was the recipient of the 1981 President's Award from the Christian Film Distributors Association.

Any speaking engagement requests or inquiries concerning Joyce Landorf Heatherley books, tapes, and music may be directed to 1-800-777-7949.